Oct. 15, 2017

DAD & MOM'S
COUNTRY WISDOM

To Wilma

God Bless You!

Jim

Psalm 37:25

D1598905

ENDORSEMENTS

JIM HAS BEEN A GODLY faithful friend for many years. He has been a great blessing to me and to our ministry. So often in our conversations we have journeyed down country roads, climbed through hay filled barns, and stopped to learn the lessons from God's wonderful creation. His book is a delightful return to times and places when simple but profound lessons from God can be learned.

George Grossman
Pastor, Walnut Street Baptist Church

WHAT COULD BETTER DESCRIBE THE character of this unique book than the phrase, a country boy and his Bible? Jim Geyer, at heart, is a farm boy from Indiana. He grew up "bustin' sod and milkin' cows." The farm was first in his life until he took the Lord Jesus as his Savior. Then his passion for Christ outgrew his dedication to the land. His care for animals became tenderness for the Lord's sheep. This book exhibits the union of rural wisdom and biblical understanding. If you enjoy the country and you love the Lord, you will be blessed by this book.

Dr. Dennis McKinsey

SEVERAL YEARS AGO I HAD the privilege of being trained by Mr. Jim Geyer in the area of Christian school development. He is a uniquely gifted communicator, and I am forever grateful for the valuable guidance, wisdom and insight he taught me.

I recently had the privilege of being one of the first to read his new book and I thoroughly enjoyed it! It is packed full of wonderful stories of his experience of growing up on a farm and the valuable lessons God taught him. He has long reflected on these lessons and finally penned them in a very interesting, thought-provoking and sometimes humorous way. His writing style takes one back to that time and place on the farm. The best part of each chapter is the spiritual application he learned through his farm experience which he so beautifully expresses to the reader. It was a blessing to me and I pray it will be to you as well!

Mrs. Sheila Smith
Development Director, Chestertown Christian Academy

WHEN I THINK OF JIM Geyer, I think of a friend of Christian education. Jim has spent much of his life as an administrator or consultant to Christian schools. I first met Jim in the capacity of a consultant, trying to help small schools survive and then to be successful. Much of the success that we have been able to enjoy at our Christian school goes back to Jim's instruction.

It didn't take long once you met Jim to know that he grew up on a farm. He seemed to always have fond memories of the farm. I would say that God was the only one that could have got Jim to leave the farm. In his book, Jim has combined his best memories with his knowledge of God's Word. The result is a practical down to earth understanding of God's principles of life. It makes for light enjoyable reading but is filled with amazing lessons about how great our God really is. May you be blessed as you read Jim's book.

Joseph Baugher
Principal, Chestertown Christian Academy

Dad & Mom's Country Wisdom
Everything I Know about the Bible
I Learned Down on the Farm

Printed in the United States of America

ISBN: 978-1-62020-031-5
eISBN: 978-1-62020-032-2

Cover Design, Page Layout & Illustrations by Matthew Mulder

AMBASSADOR INTERNATIONAL
Emerald House
427 Wade Hampton Blvd.
Greenville, SC 29609, USA
www.ambassador-international.com

AMBASSADOR BOOKS
The Mount
2 Woodstock Link
Belfast, BT6 8DD, Northern Ireland, UK
www.ambassador-international.com

The colophon is a trademark of Ambassador

Dad & Mom's
COUNTRY WISDOM

Everything I Know about the Bible I Learned on the Farm

Jim Geyer

Ambassador International
Greenville, South Carolina & Belfast, Northern Ireland

www.ambassador-international.com

Acknowledgments

Thank you Bonnie McKinsey, who patiently read my "scribblings" as she typed the original manuscript. Also, thanks to the family members and many friends who encouraged me to write this book.

This books is dedicated to my children, grandchildren and great-grandchildren, who are God's blessing to me and a source of joy.

In Memory of
Godly parents, Llyod and Mary Jane Geyer, who shaped my life for His honor and glory.

My wife of 57 years, Eleanor Jane, a farm girl whom God gave to me to encourage, support, love and complete.

CONTENTS

INTRODUCTION

"**M**y corn flakes come from a box my mom bought at a grocery store."

This response came from a nine-year-old boy after I had asked a group of school-age children the question, "From where do your corn flakes come?" I was about to show them a field of corn at the Roper Mountain Science Farm where I occasionally volunteer my time and expertise. As I quizzed the group of twenty students, only one child knew that corn flakes came from corn, but even he had no idea what a corn stalk looked like.

Among both our children and adults, ignorance of where our food comes from abounds. At the beginning of the nineteenth century, over sixty percent of the population were either living on a farm or had a garden. Today, less than one percent actually live on and work a farm, with less than five percent of our population having any kind of garden.

I had the sacred privilege of being raised on a large farm in the Midwest. As I reflect back upon my heritage, I realize it was a God-given blessing. During my childhood and early adult years, my roots went deep into God's created earth. Now from those roots has blossomed a deep love for, and fuller understanding of, God's Word; a knowledge of God's marvelous creation of the soil, trees, plants, herbs, and flowers; and an understanding of God's creation being one beautiful bloom of harmony and productivity. From this heritage has come not only a better and deeper understanding of God's Word and biblical principles but also a deeper understanding of how it has spiritually affected my life.

I believe that every aspiring pastor, regardless of the area of pastorate to which he is called, should spend at least one year on a farm. Every child should have the opportunity to spend at least one summer on a farm. This would provide each one with a better understanding of Scripture and, as a bonus, our source of food.

In Job 12:7-9 (KJV), we read that the earth and its inhabited creatures can teach us. "O speak to the earth, and it shall teach thee..." (vs. 8).

Many of the major characters of the Bible were farmers. The first garden was the Garden of Eden, cared for by Adam, the first farmer. Noah was a farmer. Job was an immensely wealthy farmer. Abraham and Isaac were prosperous farmers, while Jacob (Israel) became the first of many of the nation of Israel's farmers. Pharaoh's dream, interpreted by Joseph, was about grain and food, i.e., "Egyptian corn flakes." Ruth married a farmer (Boaz). David spent his early adult years as a sheep farmer. Uzziah, a godly king, loved the soil and farming (II Chronicles 26:10). The prophet Amos was a sheep farmer (Amos 1:1).

The Book of Psalms is like a theater—where the audience (reader) is treated to a spectacular show of both the Creator God and His works: a most pleasant green pasture field; a vast garden where we see all kinds of beautiful, fragrant flowers; a therapeutic garden to refresh both body and soul.

Ten of the thirty parables Jesus used to teach were rooted in the soil, plants, trees, and animals. Many of His illustrations and examples were of the (His) creation around Him.

Many of our country's Founding Fathers lived on a farm or were directly connected to one, e.g., George Washington, Thomas Jefferson, and others. Some (or perhaps all) of the biblically-based principles found in our country's Constitution may have been learned as our nation's Founding Fathers became and were stewards of God's rich earth and its abundant produce, including freedoms to grow and produce in all areas of life.

Dr. Paul Brand, in his book God's Forever Feast states, "Earth and Soil are so wonderful in concept and design that it is not surprising that those who live close to the earth, and farm it for food, sometimes develop a mystical sense that soil is life" (Page 67).

SOIL IS LIFE! It is from soil (dust) we came, and apart from Jesus' return, it is to the soil we will return. Hallelujah! God has done it again. He has taken a mass of lifeless earth, breathed into it the Spirit of Life, and you and I have had many years to breathe, to live, to think, to love, to produce, and to create.

God speaks to us through two sources: the written Word of God (the Bible) and the marvelous masterpiece of creation. I learned much from the masterpiece of creation that helped me understand more fully His written Word. With great hope, I trust as you read about my learning experiences that you will become a better "farmer" of both God's Word and creation. Although you may not live on an actual farm with real soil, you can become a farmer of spiritual soil, a sower of spiritual seed.

As you have driven by or visited a farm, you may have remembered some passage of Scripture. You saw a green pasture with contented cattle lying therein, and you thought of the Twenty-Third Psalm, where we are told God can lead us to "green pastures of contentment." The same was perhaps true when you saw a bountiful harvest of grain being stored in a silo or grain bin, and you thought of God wanting us to bring our "first fruits" to His storehouse.

The following pages contain many of the biblical truths and principles I learned from God's creation either consciously or subconsciously as I grew up in an agricultural environment. They also show the contrast between the moral and social culture of the past and today. It is markedly different. How marvelous are our teachers—the Holy Spirit and God's Word. May the following stories help you grow in God's Word.

JOYFUL, JOYFUL, WE ADORE THEE

All Thy works with joy surround Thee,
Earth and heaven reflect Thy rays,
Stars and angels sing around Thee,
Center of unbroken praise.
Field and forest, vale and mountain,
Flowery meadow, flashing sea,
Chanting bird and flowing fountain,
Call us to rejoice in Thee.
      —*Henry van Dyke*

KEEPING YOUR FEET UNDER GOD'S TABLE

"PASS THE FRIED CHICKEN, PLEASE"

". . . Write 'Blessed are those who are invited to the marriage supper of the Lamb.'"

Revelation 19:9 (NAS)

With a loud banging, clanging noise, the slop jar went rolling across the dining room floor, through the door into the living room, and finally came to rest against the far wall. As I climbed the stairs to my bedroom, I knew that if Dad and Mom had not been awake before, they were now, for sure. With a sinking feeling, I knew I was in trouble. It was 4:30 a.m. on a Sunday morning.

It all began with a Saturday night date with a lovely young lady who would eventually become my wife. It was a fun evening, ending around midnight with a kiss. While driving home, I passed through our small, country town. It was a one-stoplight, one-main-intersection town. As I pulled up to the stoplight (in my 1952 Chevrolet Bel Air), I saw a former high school classmate and friend, Buck Hoover, sitting on one of the benches near the intersection. Just a few months earlier, we had graduated from Madison Township High School. I pulled my car into a parking spot and joined my friend on the bench; it was a pleasant summer evening, ripe for reminiscing.

Soon another of our classmates, one who was dating a local girl, joined us. We spent the next three-and-a-half hours talking about our girlfriends, past school activities, weather, farming, future plans, freedom from teachers and studies—just about everything normal eighteen-year-olds who had just graduated from high school would discuss (and embellish).

Finally realizing the lateness of the hour, I parted company with my friends. When I turned onto the gravel road leading to my home, I turned off the headlights and slowly traveled the quarter mile to my house. I coasted into the yard and quietly tiptoed inside. Carefully and quietly closing the screen door behind me, I stealthily made my way through the kitchen and into the dining room.

Then it happened! I kicked the slop jar and sent it rolling with a noise that would have awakened the dead. I was not aware that my younger brother, Fred, had an upset stomach earlier in the evening. In order to keep a close watch on him, Mom and Dad had made a bed in the dining room, which is next to their bedroom, and had placed the slop jar next to his bed in case he vomited suddenly. Because of all my noise, Mom and Dad (and even the neighbors) knew what time I had come home. Mom always said nothing good happened after midnight, and it was far past midnight.

In case you are of the younger generation and don't know what a slop jar is (also known as a chamber pot), it is an enameled pot about three or four gallons in size that comes with a lid. It was placed in a bedroom for use by those who needed a "toilet" during the night. Of course, it was emptied the next morning. These were necessary and popular before homes had inside plumbing and toilets; outhouses served as the family toilet back in the day.

An hour later, Dad called me to get up and help with chores as usual. After chores were done, we ate breakfast. Mom and Dad never said a word about my 4:30 a.m. arrival home. With a glimmer of hope, I thought that no mention would be made of my late hours.

Then it was off to church. I know Mom and Dad were hoping for a "hellfire and brimstone" sermon about staying out most of the night. After church, Mom had prepared a scrumptious, mouth-watering meal. After we were all seated at the table, and before prayer, my Dad looked at me and said, "Son, do you like putting your feet under this table?" I looked around at the grain-fed fried chicken, fresh garden vegetables, homemade bread with fresh churned butter, and of course one of Mom's prize-winning desserts.

"Dad, of course I like living and eating here," I replied.

With a steadiness in his voice and eye, Dad said, "If you expect to keep your feet under this table, then you will keep earlier hours."

That was all he said, but what a spiritual lesson he taught me: the truth that if we want to keep "our feet under God's table," we must also live by His rules.

The Psalmist asked the questions, "Lord, who may dwell in your sanctuary? Who may live on your holy hill" (Psalm 15:1, NIV)? He goes on to answer the questions with an eleven-fold description of the righteous man who is upright in deed, word, attitude, and finances (vs. 2-5).

In Luke 22:28-30, Jesus clearly states to His disciples that they will join Him at "His table" because they have been faithful to Him through trials and temptations.

Revelation 19:7-9 tells us that only the faithful and righteous will be able to put "their feet under the table" at the glorious marriage supper.

Dad, in his country wisdom, taught me both a physical and spiritual truth that have lasted me a lifetime.

When Dad laid down his rules, my first thought was, "Wait just a minute, Dad! I am eighteen, a high school graduate, have my own car, and, and, and . . . should be able to come and go as I please." But Dad's steady, firm look kept me from getting into further trouble. Aren't we the same way in our reactions to God's rules? We know we are in the wrong and God is right, yet we want to argue or even ignore His right to discipline and guide our lives, regardless of our age, education, profession, etc.

God has a forever, eternal feast prepared for us, spread on heaven's table. By obedience to and love for God and His eternal Word, we can "put our feet under His table" forever.

Do you have your feet under God's table?

ACCOUNTABILITY

"The Corn Field Caper"

He who conceals his sins does not prosper, but whoever confesses and renounces them finds mercy,

Proverbs 28:13

"Jim, there is someone here to see you."

There was irritation in Dad's voice as he called up the stairway that led to my bedroom. Groggily, I looked at the alarm clock. It was 12:30 a.m. Just an hour earlier, I had come home from an evening spent with my longtime friend, Buck.

Now Dad's irritated voice had awakened me out of my first sleep. Slowly, I dressed and went downstairs to the kitchen where Dad awaited. There I came face-to-face with a county deputy sheriff and our local, rural hometown policeman.

"Did you earlier this evening knock over some of the corn shocks on the Wittmer brothers' farm?" asked the deputy sheriff.

I looked at Dad, who had a most stern look on his face. "Son, tell the truth; I want nothing less."

With a sinking feeling, I knew there was no escape. Both policemen wore big guns and looked like they were irritated to be out at 12:30 in the morning, when they could have been home in bed.

"Yes, Buck and I did knock over the corn shocks," I meekly responded.

After negotiations between the police, Dad, and myself, it was agreed that I would go to the Witttmer farm and stand the corn shocks back up. If I did this (along with Buck), the Wittmer brothers would not file charges against us.

The rest of the night was a restless, little-sleep night as I tossed and turned. I knew that not only would I have to spend a couple of hours standing up the corn shocks, but I also had to face Dad's wrath.

It had all begun earlier in the evening. Buck and I had gone to our country hometown to get something to eat (and look for girls). While seated in the restaurant, we got the idea it would be fun to knock over some corn shocks.

In the fall, usually October, some farmers would cut their mature corn with a binder. It would then bundle the single stalks into a bundle of ten to twenty. These bundles, fifteen to twenty of them, would then be placed in a tri-pod fashion. It was fun to run at full speed to see if the tri-pod of bundles could be knocked over. Sometimes it would take two of us running as fast as we could to knock over a shock.

While standing in the tri-pod shock, the ears of corn would finish drying and be ready to be husked sooner. Lying on the ground, however, the ears would be more apt to retain moisture and rot. Those were consequences that we did not stop to consider.

After Buck and I had finished discussing our plans, we left the restaurant and went to the place we had chosen for our evening's entertainment—the Wittmer farm. Unbeknownst to us, one of the waitresses had overheard our plans and alerted the town policeman, who then alerted the deputy sheriff.

When we arrived at the Wittmer farm, we slowly drove by the front of the farm. Imagine our surprise when we saw a deputy sheriff's car sitting in one of the farm's driveways!

"Buck, why do you suppose that deputy sheriff is sitting there?" I asked.

"I think he is just watching for speeders," Buck replied.

As we traveled down the road, discussing whether or not we should abandon our planned escapade, we decided to go ahead with it. After all, the corn field was about a half mile away from the deputy sheriff's car, and we could use a side road to the backside of the field. Turning off the headlights, we turned around and cautiously, slowly drove to the backside of the field.

After running fast, hitting and knocking over several shocks with great satisfaction, we headed back to the car and home. Because it was a dark night (starlight alone was enough to see the outline of the shocks), we knew no one had seen us.

Now our actions had been found out. The only satisfaction I had was that Buck and I had pulled off the corn shock caper right under the deputy sheriff's watch.

In the morning, after the chores were done and breakfast eaten, Dad took me out of the house. As we stood in the shade of a giant oak tree, he said, "Son, you will go to the Wittmers and apologize first and then carefully set up their corn shocks." He paused and then continued. "Your sins have found you out, and now it is time for accounting and restitution. Even if no one knew it was Buck and you, God knew. Even if there was no accounting and restitution on the earth, one day there would be an accounting before God."

With his sober reminder, I headed to the Wittmers.

When I drove into their front yard, they were waiting with arms crossed and stern looks. Dad had called to tell them that I was on my way. After profusely and humbly apologizing, I started for the corn field. One of the brothers stopped me and said, "Jim, you don't need to set up the shocks. The weather has been very dry, and we are about to start husking the corn out of shocks. It would be better to just leave them lay."

That day I learned not only about accountability, I learned about mercy.

In today's permissive culture, there seems to be little individual responsibility and accountability. Spouses cheat on their wives or husbands and then try to cover and hide their infidelity. When caught, as they usually are, they offer excuses rather than apologies.

Children who try to hide their sin from their parents, when caught in their sinful actions, rebel with anger rather than remorse and sorrow. Employees who cheat their employers by stealing time, materials, and money, offer flimsy excuses and drift on to the next employer when caught. Students caught cheating on exams or homework are excused with little punishment by both parents and teachers.

In today's society, most parents have failed to teach their children individual responsibility and accountability. Businesses fail to aggressively hold accountable and prosecute shoplifters and the employees who steal from them. Because of the time and money it takes to prosecute internal or external theft, businesses just allow an individual to be irresponsible with no restitution or accountability.

A study of many men and women in the Bible reveals that God holds people individually responsible and accountable—Adam lost his membership in the Garden of Eden Club. Noah got drunk and fathered a nation that was long a thorn in the side of Israel. David committed adultery and murder, and his family members paid a heavy price, including deception and more murder. Solomon allowed his many wives to turn his heart from God, and his kingdom was divided.

Thankfully, the corn field caper continued my education in individual responsibility and accountability. Parents and teachers, are you teaching your children, your students, individual responsibility and accountability? If not, start today.

THISTLES AND THORNS

"OUCH! THORNS ARE SHARP!"

"Cursed is the ground because of you; through painful toil you will eat of it all the days of your life. It will produce thorns and thistles for you . . ."

Genesis 3:17-18

Grrinngg! Grrinngg! That sound stopped me in my tracks and sent despair into my heart. Dad was in the shop, sharpening the hoes and maybe a spade. I knew it would only be a few minutes before Dad, my two brothers, and I would be in the pasture field, hoeing out those dreadful, pesky, awful thistles.

The thunderstorm had rolled like a mighty ocean wave over the farm the previous afternoon. It was the typical summer thunderstorm with lightning, thunder, heavy dark clouds hanging low to the ground, and copious amounts of rain. The rain had slowed to just a steady rain by nightfall, and sometime during the night, it had stopped altogether. Now the rain droplets on the leaves and grass sparkled like diamonds in the morning sun, and the ground was soaked, which would make hoeing the thistles easier.

We had arisen early, as usual. The morning chores were completed; the delicious, large country breakfast of fresh eggs, homegrown bacon, fried potatoes, homemade bread, jelly, and fresh fruit from our orchard had been eaten; I was on my way to the barn to play in the tunnels made of bales of straw when I heard that dreadful sound.

My two brothers and I tried to hide, but Dad—being wise in the ways of boys—knew all of our hiding places. He certainly would not accept our excuses of feeling sick due to some new, mysterious, exotic bug that was about to strike us, causing headaches, stomach aches, diarrhea (and maybe even death).

Soon, like a small army of soldiers, Dad had us marching toward the pasture field with our "weapons" over our shoulders. He assembled us in a line, and we each were responsible to chop down the thistles on either side of us for ten to twelve feet. When we reached the far end of the field, we moved over our assigned distances and started back, hoeing out those dreaded thistles as we went.

The summer sun was hot. I was sweating and under my breath was cursing Adam for causing this dreadful situation I was experiencing. In Genesis 3:17-18, God stated, "Adam, among many other things, because you sinned, you will be hoeing thistles." Now I was hoeing thistles. I had already learned in Sunday school about Adam's sinful "shortcomings." To me, Adam was just about the worst person I had ever heard of or known. Then my disgust with Adam was shifted to some of my neighbors, the railroad right-of-way that bordered one end of the pasture field, and the roadsides.

We always cut the thistles before they could go to seed and grow anew. But some of the neighbors, and certainly the railroad and road departments, let thistles grow and go to seed. Now the seeds had been blown by the winds into our pasture field, and I was paying the price for their negligence.

"Dad, Fred (my youngest brother) is not hoeing his share of the distance between us. Make him do his share." Dad would remind me that I was older and stronger and should carry more of the load. So, I went back to thinking bad thoughts about Adam, my neighbors, and the railroad.

"Dad, why can't we just let the thistles grow? After all, thistle blossoms are a pretty purple, and the cattle have plenty of grass to eat." Dad would then patiently explain that in a short period of time the thistles, left uncut, would crowd out the grass; if the cattle had little or no grass, they would soon stop producing meat and milk. Now, the idea of no milk sounded good, since I despised milking the one cow we had.

Dad, who seemed able to read my mind, reminded me that without meat there would be no thick steaks, no meat loaf (Mom made the best), and no juicy hamburgers. Without milk there would be no rich, thick cream for butter, nor would there be any milk for Mom to make her delectable desserts. So I toiled on, cutting those pesky thistles, not realizing the invaluable spiritual lessons I was learning through "painful toil," the legacy and reality of Adam's Fall.

With sweat dripping off the end of my nose, I continued to despise every thistle I saw. Almost with a vengeance, I attacked each one.

"Son, be glad I sharpened the hoes. A sharp hoe cuts much quicker and easier." Subtly, Dad had taught me a beginning spiritual lesson from Hebrews 4:12, which states, "For the Word of God is living and active, sharper than any double-edged sword; it penetrates even to dividing soul and spirit, joints and marrow, it judges the thoughts and attitudes of the heart."

As I progressed through life, I learned the best way to remove the "thistles of sin" which cause spiritual unfruitfulness was to use a sharp tool: the Word of God.

Later in life, as I gained an understanding of Scriptures as well as wisdom from experience, I realized I had learned another valuable spiritual lesson from the pasture field—the curse remains. Every time a thistle or thorn sprouts and grows, it is a reminder of God's curse upon the original sin of Adam and Eve. Although the original pronouncement took place thousands of years ago, it is still visible today. Those pesky thistle seeds apparently survived the great flood of Noah's time, a true demonstration of just how tough it is to keep thistles out of a physical field—or a spiritual heart.

Even as there is visible proof of the truth in all of the pronouncements in Genesis 3:16-19 —. . . in woman's sorrow in bringing forth children; man being condemned to exhausting labor in order to make a living, the body returning to dust—so also thistles are living proof of the infallibility of God's Word.

The curse is again spoken of in Genesis 5:28 and 29, "When Lamech had lived 182 years, he had a son. He named him Noah and said, 'He will comfort us in the labor and painful toil (emphasis mine) of our hands caused by the ground the Lord has cursed.'" I could relate to Lamech. I, like him, wanted relief from the "thistle problem."

Thistles don't produce fruit. The pretty, purple blossoms on a thistle look so inviting, yet the thorns are so sharp. The thorns kept the cattle from eating the thistles and the grass close to it. Thistles left to multiply soon not only crowd out the grass, but also don't produce any "fruit."

To illustrate how to know false teachers from true teachers, Jesus said, in the Sermon on the Mount, it is by the "fruit" they produce. "By their fruit you will recognize them. Do people pick grapes from thornbushes or figs from thistles?" (Matthew 7:15 [emphasis mine])

Finally, the task of removing the thistles from the pasture field was done. We wearily headed to the house for dinner. (On the farm, the noon meal was "dinner" and the evening meal was "supper.") Mom had sensed that we would need a little encouragement, so she prepared our favorite foods with an extra helping of her award-winning desserts. Dad would give us the afternoon to play as we wished or take us on a special trip to town.

As I reflected upon Mom and Dad's "rewards" for our "painful toil," I have come to realize that God treats us in the same way. He rewards us so abundantly with "shady green pastures (with no thistles) beside the still waters" when we faithfully, and sometimes painfully, toil for Him.

Is your heart filled with spiritual thistles and thorns, crowding out the fruits of God's blessings and your service and faithfulness to Him? Or is the "soil" of your heart soft and fertile from which grows an abundance of spiritual fruit? The choice is yours.

I went past the field of the sluggard, past the vineyard of the man who lacks judgment; thorns had come up everywhere; the ground was covered with weeds, and the stone wall was in ruins. I applied my heart to what I observed and learned a lesson from what I saw; A little sleep, a little slumber, a little folding of the hands to rest— and poverty will come on you like a bandit and scarcity like an armed man.

Proverbs 24:30-34

THE BLESSINGS OF SNOW

"LET IT SNOW! LET IT SNOW! LET IT SNOW!"

Hast thou entered into the treasures of the snow?
or hast thou seen the treasures of the hail....

Job 38:22 (KJV)

SCRUNCH! SCRAPE! RUMBLE! RATTLE! I awoke with a start. "Oh, no, it's the dreaded snow plow! Now I'll have to go to school in the morning." It was 2:00 a.m. The snow plow was clearing the roads of the deep snow drifts.

The snow began three days earlier with dark, ominous clouds moving toward us. Soon it was snowing. For twenty-four hours, it snowed furiously. The winds at forty to fifty miles per hour whipped and whirled the snow into huge drifts as high as eight feet! Even in midday, it was so dark it seemed almost night. Only the whiteness of the snow gave some light. It was a real blizzard!

After a day, the storm subsided. The morning light revealed a totally white landscape, with the drifts blocking the roads from any kind of travel. As I gazed upon this "heaven-sent miracle," I knew it would be a while before I would be able to go back to school.

Then the snow fun began with two days of pleasure—two days of playing in the deep snow and drifts. My siblings, the neighbor kids, and I played fox and geese, a great snow game (I am not sure where the name of this game came from; I never saw fox and geese playing in the snow), built snow forts, had snowball fights, built tunnels in and through the deep drifts, flew down the barn hill on our sleds, and made snow angels. Mom made lots of hot chocolate with marshmallows and homemade cookies for us when we came into the house to warm up. Why, she and Dad even joined us in some snow games! The snowstorm was a great blessing to bring us together as a family. We played together in the snow and also worked together as one to meet the needs of the livestock.

It was not easy taking care of the livestock and doing the chores during the three days of the blizzard and its results. It took a lot of extra effort just to get the doors to the livestock barns open and feed the many animals that depended upon us for their well-being. It took an hour of shoveling just to get from the house to the main barn. It seemed like Dad spent most of the three days just shoveling snow so we could feed and water the livestock.

The merchants in the nearby towns complained about being unable to sell their merchandise since no one could get to their stores.

During my lifetime, I have heard far more complaints about snow than the blessings of snow. There are many blessings to be found in snow. There are twenty-five references to snow in Scripture, and all are positive. God gave us these twenty-five Scripture verses to remind us of Him and what He has done for us.

Three of the first four references are found in Exodus 4:6, Numbers 12:10, and 2 Kings 5:27, which deal with the color of leprous skin being "white as snow." In two of these three references, both Moses and Miriam were miraculously healed. These verses speak of God's judgment followed by a miracle. Five of the twenty-five (twenty percent) are found in the book of Job. These verses should remind us of God's judgment on sin, our sin, and how we are miraculously pardoned from the sin curse by the blood of Jesus Christ. Job 9:30 speaks of the cleansing effect of "snow water." In 24:19, Job points out that snow water is a restraining against and being opposite of "heat and drought." In 37:6 we are told that it is God who sends the snow, and 38:22 is the classic of all snow references. In this part of God's speech to Job, He asks the question, "Hast thou entered into the treasures of the snow?" Treasures in the snow! —such as I found as a boy.

In Psalm 51:7, David wants his heart and life to be clean and pure again, like snow. Snow can be a symbol of God's cleansing and forgiveness in our hearts. In Psalm 147:16 and 148:8, God tells us He is in command of nature, including snow.

In Isaiah 1:18, God tells us that our hearts were brightly glaring with sin, scarlet and crimson, but by His redeeming love, our hearts are as white as snow. Oh, how snow should remind us of God's great love for sinners.

In Isaiah 55:10, we are reminded how God uses rain and snow to water the earth, nourishing the plants for our daily blessing of food.

In Matthew 28:3, Mark 9:3, and Revelation 1:14, the clothing of an angel and Jesus is compared to the whiteness of snow. Snow should remind us of purity, being pure, and of the power and majesty of angels, Jesus, and God.

As a boy, I found the physical and emotional treasures in the snow. As an adult, I have found the spiritual treasures in the snow. It reminds me of God's miraculous, healing power; His cleansing and forgiveness of our sins, making our hearts white as snow; His total command of nature; His provision of our daily bread; and of His purity and power. No wonder God asked Job the question, "Hast thou entered into the treasures of snow?"

The writers of The One Year Book of Psalms (December 7) do an excellent, practical summary of the blessings of snow:

"To the psalmist, snow was an amazing creation of God—as it is today. In the book of Job, when God boasts about all he has made, he includes snow (Job 38:22). Many of us marvel that no two snowflakes are made exactly alike, and we should, but snow is not just decorative. God also uses snow to purify the air, insulate the ground, and provide a slow supply of water to percolate to underground water reserves.

"But even more remarkable is the fact that God can make us 'as clean as freshly fallen snow' (Isaiah 1:18). Impurities fill our world and even our own hearts, but God blankets us with his grace, covering us with a blanket of white wool donated by the Lamb of God."

Have you found treasures in the snow? The next time it snows, don't complain . . . just go find the treasures in the snow!

SASSAFRAS TEA

"A Cure for All That Ails You"

And God said, "Let the earth bring forth grass, the herb yielding seed, and the fruit tree yielding fruit after his kind whose seed is in itself, upon the earth;" and it was so. And the earth brought forth grass, and herb yielding seed after his kind, and the tree yielding fruit, whose seed was in itself, after his kind; and God saw that it was good.

Genesis 1:11-12 (KJV)

"Dad, when you and the boys go to the woods to cut wood, bring some roots from the sassafras tree. It is time for our spring tune-up."

These were the parting words from Mom as we hurried out the kitchen door. It was early spring, and there were still patches of snow on the ground. The wood supply for both the cooking stove and furnace had been depleted. The hearty country breakfast had been eaten. We had put on our warm coats and caps, and as we started to leave, Mom's words came flying after us.

Oh, no, I thought, not sassafras tea time. I would much rather have a cup of coffee, hot chocolate, or milk than sassafras tea. Why make us suffer? We have been good kids. Why punish us with sassafras tea? These were my thoughts as we piled the axes, saws, and so forth onto the wagon. "Maybe Dad will forget to bring the roots back to Mom," I mused.

Soon we were in the woods, cutting up some fallen trees. Within a few hours, the wagon was piled high with wood from our labors. It was time to get back to the house to unload.

Then it happened—Dad remembered. Picking up a shovel, he walked to a nearby sassafras tree and dug up some roots for Mom. Under the canopy of large trees in the woods, the sassafras tree usually is a smaller tree (of the laurel family) and is originally native to the New England and upper Midwest states. It can reach a height of thirty-five to forty feet and is noted for its beautiful spring leaves of yellow and green, and its fall colors of brilliant oranges and reds.

If I had been born a cowboy on a western ranch, I would have escaped the torture of sassafras tea. No escaping now ... sassafras tea was in our near future. Mom would take the roots, dry them, and then peel the bark, crush it, and put the crushed bark in water for a day or so. Then the water would be heated and served in cups. Mom believed that this herbal type of drink was necessary to revive the body after a long winter. She believed it was a tonic that would kill any leftover, evil bacteria or viruses from winter. She also believed it would revive and spark our very souls from the clutches of the winter doldrums.

"Mom, I can't drink this tea. See, there are nasty bugs in it," I pleaded as I pointed out the tiny bits of bark that were swimming in my tea.

"Drink it," Mom commanded. "It is good for what ails you."

I didn't know anything was ailing me. But, if Mom said so, it must be true; Moms don't lie. Why, some folks (adults, of course, not us discerning kids) drank it on a regular basis.

It seemed like spring couldn't officially arrive until we had drunk a cup of sassafras tea each day for several days. Many decades later, few people realize that the ritual of drinking sassafras tea heralded the arrival of spring.

God's creation of plants was, and still is, perfect. Every plant man would need to be "healthy, wealthy and wise," God created,

including the sassafras tree. Plants furnish not only food for man and animals, but also health and well being.

Before World War II, most of our medicines came from plants, especially herbs. Purple long-stemmed digitalis, what we enjoy and is commonly known as foxglove, is a heart medicine. Purple Echinacea, known as the coneflower, is used as a sedative and relaxant. Bee balm's crushed leaves were used to relieve stings and bites. Lamb's ears (the original bandage) was used to cover and heal wounds, and the list could go on and on.

Our ancestors used plants for not only medicinal purposes, but also culinary, aromatic, and dye purposes. After World War II, many of the manufacturing plants that had produced millions of tons of munitions and explosives turned to manufacturing pharmaceuticals. Although still available today are many medicines made from plants, many more are manufactured from chemicals. This is not to say medicines made from other than plant sources are bad. As a ten-year-old boy (1944), my life was saved by the newly-discovered penicillin when my appendix ruptured. Thank goodness there is today a growing interest in returning, as much as possible, to the plants that God perfectly made, plants that meet all of our nutritional and health needs. This is evident in the growing number of health food stores.

At the time of the writing of this chapter, there is a major debate going on about health care reform. Costs of health care have skyrocketed. However, 75-80 percent of all health care problems could be eliminated by following the biblical commands of:

- thinking right – filling our minds with pure, godly thoughts

- eating right – filling our bodies with only right amounts of right food
- resting right – allowing our bodies to get regular rest

Spiritually, the gospel brings salvation. Mentally, applying God's Word to our lives promotes a sound mind. Physically, the good news is that God has provided many great plants for our healthy well being.

The ten leading causes of doctor visits, hospitalization, and insurance claims include obesity, diabetes, hemorrhoids, heart attacks, diverticulosis, cancer, peptic ulcer, hiatal hernia, appendicitis, and gallstones. These could be sharply reduced by proper thinking, eating, and resting.

Herbs and other plants are one of God's many special blessings. In many ways they link us to the living reality of the Bible and our ancestors.

Sassafras tea: was it good for me? Did it take care of all that ailed me? I don't know, even to this day. What I do know is that sassafras was created by God, and His creation is perfect.

THE BREVITY OF LIFE

"I Got There In a Hurry"

You sweep men away in the sleep of death;
they are like the new grass of the morning—
though in the morning it springs up new,
by evening it is dry and withered.

Psalm 90:5, 6

Why, you do not even know what will happen tomorrow.
What is your life? You are mist that appears for a little while
and then vanishes.

James 4:14

I looked with astonishment at the withered grass. How could this be? Why, just this morning the now drying, brown, withered grass had been tall, willowy, lush, green grass. Seven hours earlier, it had been mowed in preparation for harvesting for feed. Usually it took two or even three days to dry enough for harvesting purposes. The withering and drying was expected, but so soon?

"Son, that is a perfect picture of a person's life," Dad mused as we stood at the edge of the field. "Scriptures tell us that a person's life comes and goes quickly. It is pictured as green grass in the morning and withered by evening. James portrays life as a vapor. And Job (24:2) pictures our lives as a mere shadow that comes and goes quickly."

Just then a billowy cloud passed between us and the sun. For a few brief moments we were in a shadow; then it was gone. "Like that, son," Dad continued. "The cloud illustrated my point about the brevity of life."

I started to respond to Dad's wise observation and comments with disbelief, thinking, "Right, Dad, obviously you have forgotten that I am in my teens with fifty to sixty years to go before I am old and withered. Why, I at times even have feelings of immortality." But, I didn't verbalize my thoughts; I accepted Dad's wisdom as perhaps a misunderstanding of Scripture.

The years, like migratory birds in flight, flew by with marriage, four children, building of a large farming operation, study to complete both an undergraduate and graduate degree, teaching, coaching, administration, and consulting.

And then, like a bolt of lightning, Dad's brief, philosophical question shattered our casual conversation.

"Jim, you got there in a hurry, didn't you?"

It was a sobering question that not only intently captivated my thoughts then, but has continued to keep me focused on life itself for many years since.

It all began when I was visiting my elderly dad. He was one of those who was made tough in character by both a devastating economic depression (1930s) and the frugality of life during World War II. Dad only had an eighth-grade education, like so many others of that era. Yet, always with the desire to learn, he was a self-educated farmer, carpenter, electrician, and plumber. In the midst of the most severe economic depression the country has ever known, Dad married, started a family, and bought a 160-acre farm. Out of necessity, he needed to learn to master various skills, and he did. Over the years, life's experiences had sharpened his wisdom.

Now, at the age of eighty-eight, Dad's body had deteriorated and weakened to the point that he was no longer able to work or play. Yet, his mind had remained sharp and insightful.

It was Thanksgiving time; my wife and I had volunteered to take care of Dad for a week. My sister and brother-in-law who faithfully cared for him needed some time away to visit their family members.

After a country breakfast, Dad and I retired to his living quarters. The conversation started with the usual concerns about the current farming conditions, current prices for grain, the farm's economic outlook for the next year and, as always, the weather.

I was relaxed and enjoying the time and conversation with my Dad when he asked the next question.

"Jim, you have a birthday next week, don't you?"

"Yes, Dad, I do."

"How old will you be?"

I smiled as I responded. "Now, Dad, you know how old I will be. You were there when I was born."

After a momentary chuckle, he said, "You will be sixty." He paused, reflected for a moment, and then said, "You got there in a hurry, didn't you?"

I started to respond, but then the question hit me with such force that I couldn't respond with even a nod of agreement. Immediately, my mind raced in reverse through the halls of time, back to when I was eighteen and thought that sixty was forever in the future. Me, ever being sixty? Why, sixty was an age for old people.

I thought of my starting to farm in partnership with my dad at age eighteen, my marriage at age nineteen; father of four children by age twenty-six; called into the full-time ministry at age thirty-five; completion of undergraduate and graduate degrees, grandparent at age forty-two (eventually grandparent to eleven); six years as a Christian school administrator; and several years as a consultant to Christian ministries. And wow, all of a sudden I am sixty. How could it have happened so soon? Why, it seemed like only yesterday I was graduating from high school. And now I was within ten years of God's warning and promise of "three score and ten years." As swift as a jet plane crossing the sky, over forty years of my life had flown by.

Later that day, as I walked along a quiet, country road, Dad's simple yet profound question was still in the center of my thoughts. The question, which pointed out the brevity of life, should have been no surprise to me. Dad's discerning and wise question is clearly pointed out in the oldest of Psalms—Psalm 90. From this Psalm, one is reminded of three facts of life. First, in verses three to six (KJV), one learns of the frailty of man and the brevity of life. "...they are like grass which groweth up. In the morning it flourishes, and groweth up; in the evening it is cut down, and withereth" (vs. 6).

In verses nine to eleven we are reminded of the shortness of life. "The days of our years are threescore and ten...it is soon cut off, and we fly away" (vs. 10). And in verse twelve, one is reminded of the importance of using time on earth wisely and for God's glory. "So teach us to number our days, that we may apply our hearts unto wisdom." Dad's question not only prompted many thoughts about my swiftly-passing life; it made me search my heart about my focus in life; about the use of the rest of my time that God will allot me.

As I reflected back, I realized I had learned two truths. First, I realized that not all of the time with which God had blessed me had been used wisely. Yes, Dad's probing question left me with some regrets about the past. But, his question also helped me focus anew on the future and my mission and purpose in life, serving and loving my God. Secondly, I realized that once the plant is cut off from its source of water and nutrients, it soon dies. The cutting and withering is a microcosm of life itself. Philip Gulley, in his book Front Porch Tales (page 150), describes this life scenario best.

Elton Trueblood talked about how we're a cut-flower world. We sever things from their life source and expect them to flourish. And we cut ourselves off from God and are dismayed when our lives wilt and fade. We spend so much time chasing after the baubles of the world, we're bankrupt when it comes to the treasures of the holy. We want joy and beauty, but we want them without having to stay connected to the One who gives them. So we look for them in the world but come up empty-handed and empty-hearted.

Thanks, Dad! You reminded me how quickly life passes and the importance of being a good steward of my time.

"Life is brief at best and abrupt at worst. Each day is a gift from God to be used for His glory and to experience the abundant life that He offers to those who love Him."

—Dr. Ron Stewart

HARVEST TIME

"TABLES OF FOOD – BUSHELS OF GRAIN"

Then he said to his disciples, "The harvest is plentiful but the workers are few. Ask the Lord of the harvest, therefore, to send out workers into his harvest field."

Matthew 9:37-38

The tables were laden with all kinds of delightful, delectable, delicious food: home-grown, grain-fed beef and ham piled high on huge platters; beans with bacon bits, peas with onions, squash, red beets, cabbage, and cauliflower fresh from the garden; huge pans of mashed potatoes with rich, creamy gravy; macaroni and cheese; thick slices of fresh, homemade bread on which could be spread creamy homemade butter, fresh jellies, jams, and sweet apple butter; a long table of nothing but desserts—three layer cakes with creamy frosting, pies of every description, and platters of cookies; and finally, a table loaded with containers of sweet lemonade.

I loved wheat harvest time on the farm!

It was a time of hard work; a time when farmers united together to help one another harvest their wheat crop; a time when the wives and daughters gathered to prepare the noon meal just described; and a time of great food, fellowship, and community spirit.

Before the days of the grain combine, there were groups of farmers who became a part of a threshing "gang." Usually, the gang consisted of ten to twelve farmers. One of the farmers owned the threshing machine, which consisted of a steam-powered tractor and a grain separator.

In early July, a farmer would hitch his horses to a grain binder that would cut the grain and bundle it into sheaves. The farmer then gathered ten or twelve sheaves and arranged them in a tight circle, with two or three sheaves placed on top to shed rain. By doing this, the grain ripened more evenly, and also a thunderstorm would not flatten the heavy grain-laden stalks, which would make it almost impossible to harvest and thus a crop would be lost.

A few weeks later, the threshing would begin. The farmers would draw lots to see who was first, second, and so on. The morning would begin with the threshing machine owner putting the grain separator in the right place. Then he would back the steam tractor into place. The fifty-foot endless belt was placed on the pulleys of both tractor and separator, tightened, and the day of threshing began. Two or three wagons pulled by sturdy workhorses, with two or three men per wagon, would head for the wheat field. From one bundle of sheaves to the next they would go, loading the wagons until they seemed ready to tip over. The first loaded wagon would pull up to the separator. There, two men would throw the sheaves into the hungry mouth of the separator. The separator would then separate the grain from the stalk; the grain would flow down a tube into waiting burlap sacks or wooden bushel baskets to be transported to the granary to store for future livestock feed or to be sold. The straw was blown onto a pile for future livestock bedding.

I loved to hear the steam engine's melodic sound as it labored to separate the grain from the chaff and straw. As the sweaty men used their pitchforks and threw the sheaves into the gaping mouth of the separator, the engine would respond with a deep, accelerated "chug-chug-chug," with black smoke pouring out of the smoke-stack. What a sight!—What a sound! The owner of the thresh-ing machine would walk around with his grease gun and oil can, lubricating the moving parts and, with his ever-present rag, wipe off a speck of dust here and a bit of dirt there. Once in a while, he would let me feed more wood into the firebox of that monstrous, smoke-belching, almost-human machine.

"Son, we must keep up the steam pressure, so fill that firebox with more fuel," he would say. At the time, I didn't fully under-stand how the heat from the fire heated the water to produce the steam to keep the engine running. What I did know was that he trusted me to fuel the fire in the firebox. Along with helping to keep the engine fired, I also would carry water to the men in the field, and occasionally they would let me drive one of the teams of horses as it picked up the bundles of grain.

Now it was dinner time. The whistle on the steam engine had called all the men to the feast. As the sweaty, dust-covered men washed in the large tubs of water, the wives and daughters, dressed in their colorful, decorative aprons, placed the food on the tables in the shade of the tree-filled lawn.

After one of the men led in a thanksgiving prayer, the fellowship and feasting began. I enjoyed hearing the men and women talk about politics, the weather, families, current events, and especially what would happen now that the war (WWII) had ended, just eleven months earlier.

The Bible has sixty-two references to harvesting. As I grew in knowledge of the Scriptures about harvesting, my memories would return often to the harvest time on the farm. The first time the word "harvest" is used is found in Genesis 8:22 (KJV). "While the earth remaineth, seed-time and harvest, and cold and heat, and summer and winter, and day and night shall not cease."

What a promise God made to Noah. He and his family had just descended from the ark. The Great Flood had interrupted the normal flow of the seasons, including planting and harvesting. As a boy, I had participated in the ongoing promise God had made to Noah thousands of years before.

One of the yearly feasts God ordained for His chosen people was the Harvest Feast (Leviticus 23), where the first fruits of the harvest were brought to the Tabernacle. Ruth and Naomi returned to Israel during harvest time. Part of the courtship of Boaz and Ruth took place in a barley field at harvest time.

In Proverbs, we are encouraged to learn from the ant about the importance of the harvest; also we learn how the lazy person will have no harvest to sustain his family, or even his life.

In Isaiah's great prophetic passage of the Coming Messiah (9:1-7), the joy of His Coming is compared to the great joy of a bountiful harvest.

With a sorrowful heart, Jeremiah warns Israel that an invading army would eat their harvest as part of God's judgment upon their disobedience and sins.

They will devour your harvests and food, devour your sons and daughters; they will devour your flocks and herds, devour your vines and fig trees. With the sword they will destroy the fortified cities in which you trust (Jeremiah 5:17).

In Matthew 9:37-38 (also Luke 10 and John 4), Jesus states three things about harvest: 1) God is the One who has created the plants that grow into the grain to be harvested; 2) there is a spiritual harvest of sinners that are waiting to hear the good news of the gospel that Jesus saves sinners; and 3) the mission fields are ripe and waiting for the harvester.

Finally, Revelation 14:15 tells of God's final seven judgments upon the earth—the seven bowl judgments are compared to a ripe harvest, a time when the debauchery and rebellion of man has ripened to its fullest.

Because I was able to participate as a boy in an old-fashioned harvest, the sixty-two scriptural references to harvest have a much deeper, colorful meaning.

How can we, as Christians, be harvesters? The songwriter gave us clear and easy directions:

BRINGING IN THE SHEAVES

Sowing in the morning, sowing seeds of
   kindness,
Sowing in the noontide and the dewy eve;
Waiting for the harvest, and the time of
   reaping,
We shall come rejoicing, bringing in the
   sheaves.

Sowing in the sunshine, sowing in the
   shadows;
Fearing neither clouds nor winter's chilling
   breeze;
By and by the harvest and the labor ended,
We shall come rejoicing, bringing in the
   sheaves.

Going forth with weeping, sowing for the
   Master,
Tho' the loss sustained our spirit often grieves;
When our weeping's over, He will bid us
   welcome,
We shall come rejoicing, bringing in the
   sheaves.

   —*Knowles Shaw, George A. Minor*

PARK FARM

"An Attempt to Return to the Garden of Eden"

*And the LORD God planted a garden eastward in Eden;
and there he put the man whom he had formed. And out of
the ground made the LORD God to grow every tree that is
pleasant to the sight, and good for food; the tree of life also in
the midst of the garden, and the tree of knowledge of good and
evil. And a river went out of Eden to water the garden; and
from thence it was parted, and became four heads. The name
of the first is Pishon; that is it which compasseth the whole
land of Havilah, where there is gold; and the gold of that land
is good; there is bdellium and the onyx stone. And the name
of the second river is Gihon; the same is it that compasseth
the whole land of Cush. And the name of the third river is
Hiddekel; that is it which goeth toward the east of Assyria.
And the fourth river is Euphrates.*

Genesis 2:8-14 (KJV)

"Ever since the Garden of Eden, man has attempted to re-
create the Garden of Eden in the parks he has built—
parks that provide a place of peace, rest, and quiet; a place free

from work, worry, and the demands of everyday duty; yes, even the temptations and ravages of sin."

With these words, the instructor of our landscaping class started the session. Wow! Her words rang bells and turned on light bulbs in my mind. My thoughts raced back to why I, and many millions of others, go to parks and how parks are designed. She went on to say, "Chahar Bagh is the word to describe the symbolic design that two intersecting lines create. It is the pattern referred to in the Bible in the book of Genesis, as the Garden of Eden is described.

"The oasis was the basis for many of the first gardens. It contained thirst-quenching water, cool shade, food, and a safe place to rest. Life could be sustained where these things were found. The oasis came to be equated with life and beauty; it was paradise.

"Man's earliest depictions of paradise are incorporated in the image/metaphor of the Garden of Eden (paradise). Man was placed in the garden to care for it. His disobedience precipitated his expulsion from this paradise. In gardening, and in many other endeavors, man tries to recreate/regain paradise." (Master Gardening course, Clemson University)

Her mind-stirring statements sent my thoughts beyond why I visit parks. In my mind's eye, I pictured the 160-acre farm my grandfather built, a place he named "Park Farm;" it was a place where he planted pine, cedar, white-blossom catalpa, walnut, and many other species of trees, and a place where he planted beautiful lavender lilac bushes, stately peonies, statuesque iris, cheerful lilies, and bright daffodils. He even had pastoral scenes painted on the huge country barn.

Why, he spent almost $700 creating a park-like farm! For a farmer to spend that amount of money landscaping in the 1890s was very unusual, unique, and equivalent to $30,000 or more today.

Why did Grandfather do what he did? Was he attempting to create a place of peace and rest even in the midst of daily farm activities? Sadly, the family has no written records of his thoughts—his reasons. I do know he loved to visit parks and world fairs. He visited parks in far away places like Cleveland, Chicago, and St. Louis. His father more than likely described the beautiful parks of Europe, where he was born.

Growing up, I had the pleasure of experiencing and enjoying some of the fruits of the apple and pear trees; the quiet walks through the cedar, pine, and catalpa trees; the flowering perennials; and especially the beautiful, purple-blossomed, fragrant lilacs.

During my childhood days, I wish my grandfather had been alive. I would have liked to walk with him among the trees and ask, "Why did you create a park-like farm?" No, Grandpa didn't plant a tree of "knowledge" or of "good and evil." But he did plant trees and flowers that brought much enjoyment and pleasure to future generations.

In Psalm 36:8, it states, "You feed them from the abundance of your own house, letting them drink from your rivers of delight" (emphasis mine). The word for delight in that verse is translated from the plural form of the Hebrew word for "Eden."

Grandpa, you certainly brought me, other family members, neighbors, and friends delight in the park you created. "Thy Word is like a garden, Lord, with flowers bright and fair; and everyone who seeks may pluck a lovely cluster there" (Edwin Hodder).

Although we can and do find peace and solitude in parks, we can find even greater peace and contentment in Jesus Christ. Jesus said:

"Peace I leave with you; My peace I give to you; not as the world gives, do I give to you. Let not your heart be troubled, nor let it be fearful" (John 14:27, NAS).

"These things I have spoken to you, that in Me you may have peace. In the world you have tribulation, but take courage; I have overcome the world" (John 16:33, NAS).

Paul, writing to Timothy, stated:

But godliness actually is a means of great gain, when accompanied by contentment. For we have brought nothing into the world, so we cannot take anything out of it either. And if we have food and covering, with these we shall be content (I Timothy 6:6-8, NAS).

It was in a garden, a park-like setting (Gethsemane) where Jesus sought peace concerning the heaven-sent, changing-the-world-forever event He was about to face; the peace—the courage to surrender to His Father's will—came in a garden.

". . . Father, if thou be willing, remove this cup from me: nevertheless not my will, but thine, be done" (Luke 22:42, KJV).

A few years ago, I was invited to landscape a dentist's office yard. The dentist and I agreed it should be, as much as possible, a park-like setting so that patients would be "at peace" as they came and went. PEACE AT A DENTIST'S OFFICE? A place of high speed drills, needles, and pain? But it worked, as many hundreds of patients have testified.

In all honesty, a home (backyard or patio) should be so park-like that it provides a place of peace and tranquility for family members.

Businesses are encouraged to do the same for the peace of their employees.

Although the peace of a park or garden is very good and to be desired, the peace God brings through being obedient to His Word and accepting Jesus Christ as Lord of our lives is even greater.

God has given me the privilege of having visited many local, state, and national parks. I have immensely enjoyed their beauty, solitude, and peaceful atmospheres. Beyond the parks, I enjoy even more the peace and contentment that Jesus can give in a tumultuous, distressed, evil, sin-ravaged world. Jesus can be, and is, our "Garden of Eden."

Park Farm was my first introduction to the biblical Garden of Eden. Thanks, Grandpa. Little did you know how much your creative efforts would benefit a grandson you never knew.

What are you leaving your family's future generations? Have you, Dad or Mom, provided a therapeutic garden, a "Garden of Eden," for yourself and your children?

UNCLE LEIGHTON

"FLOWERS AND TREES, BIRDS AND BEES"

The land produced vegetation: plants bearing seed according to their kinds and trees bearing fruit with seed in it according to their kinds. And God saw that it was good.

Genesis 1:12

BLAAP!

The tree branch hit me on the side of the head as I guided the combine along the edge of Uncle Leighton's wheat field. He didn't have a combine of his own, so he hired me to harvest his golden ripe grain. When I had harvested enough to fill the grain bin on the combine, I stopped to unload in the wagon waiting at the end of the field.

"Uncle Leighton, you must cut those tree limbs along the fence line. Why, one hit me so hard it almost knocked me from the combine! And while you're cutting, why don't you remove all the brush and trees in your fence lines?"

With a very serious, almost holy look upon his face, he gently responded, "Oh, I can't cut the brush and trees. They are a haven of safety and provide food for many species of birds. Also, the underbrush is a place of safety and home for the rabbits, muskrats, mink, and raccoons. Why, to remove them would take away the safe havens for God's creatures."

Seeing my suggestion had not found fertile ground in his mind, I went back to harvesting his grain. I thought, "Uncle Leighton, you sure are behind times. Why, modern farmers clean up their fence rows. Don't you know the brush and trees lower crop production along the edges of the field?"

Gently touching the growing welt on my face, I wondered if Uncle Leighton would ever be a modern farmer.

Eventually, God worked in my heart, and I learned to appreciate God's marvelous creations as Uncle Leighton did. In time I learned what a unique and special uncle I had.

Uncle Leighton was one of the most interesting uncles a person could have. His life has influenced me (and many others) in various ways for a lifetime. My love for God's miraculous creation and wonderful creatures can be directly traced to my Uncle Leighton. My eventual love for animals, flowers, trees, and all of God's marvelous and colorful creations can be traced to Uncle Leighton's teaching and example. He was a gentle person, yet firm in his beliefs. He was physically small, yet big in heart. He could whistle melodiously along with the best, yet had no formal musical training.

Uncle Leighton loved God and His Word. Each year he would read through the Bible. As he read, he would mark his favorite passages with a colored pen. Each year he would use a different color. Thus, after seven to eight years, his Bible was a multi-colored history of the Scriptures through which God spoke to him. He loved his small country church and attended faithfully for a lifetime.

He was not only faithful in attendance, but he was also faithful in his giving of both time and resources.

Like many of his generation, Uncle Leighton had only an eighth-grade formal education, yet he was a student for a lifetime. He spent many evenings studying civics, history, and the classics in literature—including Shakespeare. He was not only a student and teacher of history, he wrote family history for future family generations. He was an observant scientist who taught many about nature and life. He spent many Sunday afternoons walking in the woods, learning more about God through His creation and creatures. He was both a student and teacher of others about the birds, bees, trees, flowers, and even the weather. He loved the peace and contentment that God provided him through creation.

Uncle Leighton was noted for his beautiful flower and vegetable gardens. I vividly remember seeing him spend many hours in his gardens. As he approached the end of his life, he was only able to crawl into his gardens due to deteriorating health. A sad yet wonderful sight was to see him on his knees as he planted and enjoyed the peace and contentment that his gardens brought him.

Uncle Leighton loved music all the way from classical (Beethoven, Bach, opera, etc.) to country and western. But, his greatest love was for religious music. He loved the hymns that portrayed the holiness and majesty of God and the love of Jesus Christ, his Lord and Savior. In his later years, he watched and listened to the Lawrence Welk program every Saturday evening. This Saturday evening excursion into music became a tradition with him. So much so that any visitor to his home had to sit and watch and listen to the "bubbly" music of Lawrence Welk's orchestra with him.

After his family had left home, Uncle Leighton traveled extensively. He visited forty-nine state capitals as he traveled in forty-nine of our fifty states. At the age of ninety, he traveled with his family to Alaska. As one family member remarked, "He was the first off the boat or bus, and last to return. After others had tired, he was still exploring God's creation."

His travels began in horse-drawn buggies and wagons and ended in jet airplanes. He took his first airplane ride at age sixty-five. At age eighty-eight, from part way up Mt. Rainier, he whistled a melodious repertoire of songs that caused both humans and birds to pause and listen.

Uncle Leighton had two favorite sayings. "If you do not have time to do it right, when will you have time to do it again?" and "Is it necessary?" He believed in a strong work ethic, which he taught both by word and deed. Above all, he believed in individual responsibility along with integrity of character.

Uncle Leighton's professional life can be divided into two areas. First and foremost, he was a farmer. He worked as a hired hand for my father for several years. During this time, he lived with my parents and was like a second father to me, even buying me my first red wagon for Christmas one year.

Eventually, he bought his own farm on which he raised crops, cows, hogs, and chickens. As economic times changed and the farm was not large enough to support his family, he went to work as a carpenter. Like anything else he did, he was successful at building things with his mind and hands.

Uncle Leighton's life covered most of the twentieth century. Born in 1901 (ninth in a family of twelve), he died in 1995 at the age of ninety-four. He did not marry until he was thirty-nine years old, yet he lived to celebrate not only his fiftieth wedding anniversary, but also his fifty-fifth. Few ever accomplish this remarkable feat, especially marrying at a late age.

His life span covered the worst economic depression this country has ever known, two major world wars, and the golden ages of radio and railroading. At an early age he rode behind horses, yet he lived to see a man rocket to and walk upon the moon. He saw Haley's comet appear twice in a lifetime—a sight few can claim. He saw regular mail change to fax and then to computer, yet he handled all of these changes in technology with optimism, faith, and acceptance.

On a cold, gray December day with a wind chill well below zero, I watched as they lowered my Uncle Leighton into his physical, final resting place. Although I was "chilled to the bone," I was warmed by the memories of my relationship with him. He had been my gentle friend and teacher. I was thankful he had been my uncle.

For his friendship, I give thanks.

For his love of family and nature, I give thanks.

For his kindness and gentleness, I give thanks.

For his life, wisdom, support, I give thanks.

For his smile, I give thanks.

For his love, I give thanks.

Now many years have passed. As Uncle Leighton would say, "Much water has passed over the dam and under the bridge." Through study and understanding of God's Word, I am now teaching others verbally, in my writings, and by example how to care for God's creation. Not only how to care, but also how to appreciate God's perfect creation that daily surrounds us. Uncle Leighton, if you could see some of the gardens God has allowed me to create, you would be proud of your nephew.

In part, I have carried on Uncle Leighton's love for God's creation. Will one (or more) of my children and grandchildren carry on this great, godly heritage? I pray to that end. What about you? Are you a loving steward of God's creation?

Thanks, Uncle Leighton, for your example and patience. I know with perfect mind and health you are busy in heaven, taking care of God's garden.

> Our hearts are God's garden;
> His words are the seeds,
> His grace brings the water;
> His love pulls the weeds.
> His hand does the pruning;
> His truth is the hoe.
> His caring presence
> Makes everything grow.

From: Come Sit Awhile
The Blessings of Family & Home
Inspiration from the Front Porch
by Roy Lessin and Heather Solum

A COUNTRY CHURCH

"Small in Size, Large in Service"

*Let us not give up meeting together, as some are in the habit
of doing, but let us encourage one another—and all the more
as you see the Day approaching.*

Hebrews 10:25

Clang! Clang! Clang! Clang, Clang, Clang!
The melodic sound of our small country church bell
rang out over the countryside in a way we had not heard before.

"Mom, why are they ringing the church bell so loud and long?"
I asked. It was Sunday morning, and I was about to get ready to go
to church.

"It is because victory was declared a few hours ago in our battle
with Nazi Germany. We are celebrating Victory in Europe (VE),"
she answered.

I had often heard the church bell rung, first about one-half hour
before Sunday school began and again at the beginning of Sunday
School. Every Sunday a church member who lived close by went
early to ring the bell. The melodic ringing sound carried several
miles out from church. Its rich tones said to all the residents in our

rural community, "It is Sunday, God's Holy day; come worship the Creator of the universe and all living things with us." I could picture in my mind's eye my neighbor, who faithfully rang the 200-pound bell, just jumping up and down as he tugged on the rope that swung the bell back and forth. It was also rung on special occasions such as wedding ceremonies, funerals, etc.

Most churches built in the first part of the twentieth century were built with a steeple that housed a bell. Madison Chapel was no exception. It has a large bell that can be rung still today. A long rope came from the bell, down through the balcony, and to the main foyer. To ring the bell correctly and skillfully took practice. How thrilled I was when someone taught me to ring the bell announcing the Lord's day.

"Mom, my brothers and I are going to walk to church this morning," I announced as we finished dressing. As we walked the one-fourth mile, we talked about what the end of the war would mean. Yes, several cousins would come home. Rationing of gas, sugar, rubber tires, and so forth would cease. Families would be united, and there would be no more dread of a father or son being killed in action. It seemed that morning the sun was brighter, the birds sang sweeter, the spring flowers were prettier; why, even our family dog, Shep, was wagging his tail faster.

The church services were livelier (some of our services seemed "dead" to a ten-year-old boy) as the people rejoiced in God's answers to their many prayers. Madison Chapel's Sunday services were very special that day. In our modern vernacular, we all felt "warm and fuzzy."

Madison Chapel is just a small, country church, but it has been large in providing a spiritual haven for hundreds of souls for over a century. Located in the heart of Madison Township, St. Joseph County, Indiana, it was my home church for most of the first thirty years of my life. Vivid mental pictures and memories of Madison Chapel still abound in my heart and mind. Let me share a few of these memories with you as we walk together into the past—a past that takes us back to a time when life was more simple and yet full and rich in church and family life.

In 1906 the local residents, mostly farmers, knew that they needed a local church to meet the spiritual needs of their families and themselves . Levi Hahn, a local farmer, donated a piece of land for a church building. Some of his descendants still attend there today. Those who desired a church gathered and, with some outside carpentry and building expertise, built a church that still stands strong. Not only was the church built, but a large shed to house the horses and buggies (the mode of transportation of the time) was also added. The total cost to build the church was $2,708.10; a minute amount in comparison to the many millions that are spent building today's mega-churches.

At the time, the church was large for a rural community, since it could seat over two hundred people. It even had a large-sized balcony—which was great for teens who didn't want to sit with Mom and Dad. (However, sitting in the balcony was often not allowed by good parents.) The church was filled with wooden pews, kerosene lights (later replaced by electric lights), an old pump organ (later replaced by a piano), and an altar for repentant sinners.

Over a period of time, two renovations took place. About forty years after the church was built, the basement was expanded to improve and increase the Sunday school classrooms. Again, the work was done by members of the congregation. In the mid-1960s, a new front entrance was added, slightly enlarging the church and adding to its appearance.

By far the most important thing about the church was its rural people. The congregation was mostly comprised of hard-working, honest farm people. There were no rich folks among the body of believers; just good people who were wealthy in the spiritual treasures of heaven. It would take many pages to write about all the families who attended Madison Chapel, so I will name just a few who are most vivid in my memory.

Holley Family – The Holley family was the only black family in the church and community. They were the most colorful (no pun intended) family in the church. Hansberry Christian Holley could not read or write, but how he loved the Lord and his family! During the long winter nights, his wife, by the light of a kerosene lamp, would read Scripture to him for hours. When testimonies were requested, he would, in a loud, booming bass voice, speak boldly of God's goodness to him and his family. After a moment or two of speaking of God's love, mercy, and grace, he would burst into a stanza of his favorite song, "No, Never Alone." When Brother Holley gave his testimony, the whole church rattled. Not only were his testimonies great; his prayers were even greater. The two things I remember most about his prayers were the statements, "Lord, one day every knee will bow and every tongue confess that you are the true and living God," and "Thank you, Lord, for the air we breathe and a good night's rest." How thankful he was for the simple yet very necessary things of life. Somehow, Brother Holley knew the day was coming when the air would be polluted (smog, etc.), and it would take millions of sleeping pills to put America to sleep at night.

Brother Holley loved his family. He worked long hours to be sure his twelve children received a good education. He saw to it that they were in church every Sunday and behaved while there. When he and his family would arrive for church, the first thing he would do is walk to an apple tree growing next to the church. There he would cut a switch (about two feet long) from the tree. Then he would march his children into church, where they all sat as a family in one pew, and if any of the children misbehaved, all he had to do was raise the switch, and misbehavior ceased immediately. Thank the Lord there was no Department of Social Services at that time to "educate" Brother Holley of his wrongdoing in correcting a child's misbehavior.

In the late 1950s, Brother Holley was killed in a farming accident. Madison Chapel Church was packed for the funeral. When the obituary of one of God's great saints was read, there was not a dry eye in the church.

Stichter Family – I mention this family because of their influence on our family life. Mahlon, the father, was the music director for many years. His wife, Sarah, was noted for her constant sleeping during the preaching, regardless of how good the preacher was. Thankfully, she didn't snore. Ruth, their only child, devoted her life to her parents and teaching boys and girls about Jesus. She led many to the Lord; she was a faithful Sunday school teacher.

Geyer Family – Four generations of Geyers worshiped in Madison Chapel, beginning with my grandparents (who helped build the church), my parents, myself and my wife, and all four of our children. My Uncle Leighton worshiped there for the larger part of ninety years. My aunt, Edna Hunsberger, also worshiped there and faithfully played the piano for the services.

Madison Chapel had many pastors—some were younger; some were old; some were educated; some were God-called laymen; some were strict; some were joyful; some were expositors of God's Word; some were more narrative and practical; and for some, it was where they began their ministerial careers. But, regardless of background, education, and personality, all faithfully proclaimed God's Word.

Spring and fall revivals were an important part of church life. Twice a year there were week-long services that featured many "fire and brimstone" evangelists. Because of their God-inspired, passionate preaching, many souls were saved, and the saints were strengthened and equipped.

Another special time was the Christmas season. Each year the children, myself included, would learn our various parts for the Christmas story. Sometimes I was a shepherd, a wise man, or a father. But, the role I loved best was the year I was chosen to play Joseph. That was the "crown" in my brief acting career. I accepted my role with great seriousness and diligence. The only thing that spoiled my performance was when my beard fell off. (Maybe the biblical Joseph did not have a beard.)

Another special activity at Christmas was on the Sunday before Christmas; after the church service, each person was given a bag of various kinds of candy and an orange. How I looked forward with eager anticipation to this time. The bag of candy was one of the few times during the year when I had the "luxury" of eating sweets. How times have changed!

Prayer meetings were held every Wednesday night, and much more often during World War II. How we prayed for our nation and our armed forces. During warm weather, the prayer meetings were held in the church. During the winter months, prayer meetings were held in church members' homes due to the fact that the church was not heated during the week; at that time, the church had a wood and coal furnace. How the saints of the church could pray! They would bring heaven close with their prayers. Their prayers either lifted you into heaven or brought heaven down to you in a practical way. All prayers were offered either standing or kneeling—mostly kneeling. Sometimes during prayer, I would raise my head up to see if anyone else was looking around. Or, I would look under the pews to see if any of my friends were looking around. If they were, we would make funny faces at each other. Occasionally, an adult would look to see if the children and teens were behaving. When caught looking instead of praying, I was promptly and properly corrected of my "sin."

Most of the music was the singing of the great doctrinal and evangelical hymns. Every person had their favorite hymn; mine was "At Calvary." Even today, my heart and lips sing of the fact that, "Mercy there was great and grace was free; pardon there was multiplied to me; there my burdened soul found liberty, At Calvary" (chorus). What marvelous, biblical truths I learned as a young person. How well I remember the short Sunday school choruses of the times. The words of "Climb, Climb Up Sunshine Mountain,"

"Jesus Loves the Little Children," "Jesus Loves Me, This I Know," and others still echo in my heart today.

The greatest moment of my early church life came in the spring of 1941. As a seven-year-old boy, I gave my heart to Jesus. At a revival meeting following a fiery sermon by an evangelist about an eternal place called hell, I knew I needed a Savior.

At an altar in a small country church, surrounded by praying saints, I confessed I was lost and on my way to eternal separation from God. That night I became a child of the living God. The next morning, my mother hugged me and with tears in her eyes said, "You have made an eternal, wise decision—the best decision you will ever make." That day the sun was brighter, the grass was greener, and the birds sang sweeter.

It was also at Madison Chapel Church where, in the mid '50s, my wife was gloriously born again.

Many years have passed since my small, country church experience. I have been in many large churches, even mega-churches, and also some small ones. I have found, in some, faithful preaching of God's Word. I have felt the power of the Holy Spirit. I have seen souls saved by the power of the gospel message. I have heard the melodious songs from the hearts and lips of the choir and congregation. But nowhere have I found the unity and camaraderie I experienced in a small, country church.

I learned as a boy and young man the true meaning of Matthew 18:20 (KJV): "For where two or three are gathered together in my name, there am I in the midst of them."

God has the same power in a small church as He does in a large one. Sinners can be saved and saints edified whether the church is large or small. The gospel songwriter put it best when he wrote, "Oh, I would like to go back to that old, country church, where the glory of the Lord came down...." Although I cannot go back in time physically, I can go back in memory to a time when God often met with some good, country families. It did not take a large church with multiple associate pastors or numerous, high-powered programs for every age to meet the spiritual needs of a rural community and one boy growing up. It just took one small, country church, with wooden pews and a prayer altar, named Madison Chapel.

SHEP

"Things Have Gone to the Dogs"

And God said, "Let the land produce living creatures according to their kinds, livestock, creatures that move along the ground, and wild animals, each according to its kind." And it was so.

Genesis 1:24

My brothers and I looked with stunned silence at the broken, bloodied body of Shep, our faithful farm dog. His crumpled, lifeless body lay beside the railroad track. Only a few minutes before, we had been playing in the front yard with Shep. Now he no longer would bound with endless energy, chasing sticks, balls, rabbits, birds, and other critters and creatures. "Ol" Shep was a beautiful, lovable collie. But he had a bad habit: he loved to chase trains. When he heard an approaching train, he would race down the road or across the open field to the railroad tracks. He was not content to just watch the trains. He chased them. Dad would occasionally joke that Shep might someday drag a train that he caught into the yard, and then we would have to bury it.

Shep was not only a good companion and fun to play with, he was also a good guard dog. He helped us round up livestock when a roundup was needed. He loved to tease our farm cats. With eager eyes and a furiously wagging tail, he enjoyed riding on a wagon or in a truck. During the hot summers, he slept on the north side of the barn where it was shady and cool. During the cold winter months, he slept in the warm barn, heated by the livestock, protected from the cold winds and snow. He would lie beside us when we rested on the front porch or in the front yard.

The chasing of trains went on for years. Then, it suddenly came to an end. On that early spring day, we lost our faithful Shep. His sudden demise reminds me even today of the Scripture found in Proverbs 6:15 (KJV). "Therefore disaster will overtake him in an instant; he will suddenly be destroyed—without remedy." The speeding train created a sucking vacuum. Shep just got too close and was sucked up against the huge churning drive wheels of the engine. I think my brothers and I quoted the Twenty-third Psalm over his grave and whatever else may have come to mind in our sorrow.

In a way, Shep was an example of people who try to get as close to sin as possible without being hurt. But, like Shep, they usually are sucked into the bottomless pit of sin and ultimate demise. James, in chapter 3 verses 13 through 16, was writing his letter to warn fellow Christians of this very thing.

The Bible has forty references to dogs, most of them with a negative connotation. Often today when we refer to something that has gone wrong, we say, "Things have really gone to the dogs."

In spite of only a few positive references to dogs in Scripture, God created dogs for worthwhile purposes. They are wonderful companions to the lonely, elderly, and blind. They help farmers and ranchers round up and protect livestock. They are playful companions to children. They help policemen track down criminals who would otherwise escape. They guard businesses at night. They pull sleds and wagons loaded with goods and materials. The list could go on. Some dogs become famous movie stars, like Lassie, Bullet (Roy Rogers' dog), Beethoven (the lovable St. Bernard), and Rin-Tin-Tin. Dog antics entertain us in comic strips, such as Bitsy in the Marvin comic strip and Odie in the Garfield comic strip. They ride in parades, are mascots for athletic teams, and entertain in circuses. Dogs have been used to find and rescue people. They have alerted families in the middle of the night when a fire has broken out in a home.

In today's culture, dogs have been elevated to a level almost beyond belief. Some people have elevated them to human status. Dogs are treated as members of the family. They are pampered and spoiled beyond common sense.

Millions upon millions are spent for high-priced dog clothes: sweaters, caps, booties, and so on. They have their fur clipped and styled, and toenails trimmed by high-priced groomers. They are given special dog food. Grocery supermarkets devote two long aisles to just dog and cat food. Many dog owners treat and speak more kindly to their dogs than they do to people, including family members. Dogs are placed in expensive dog care "hotels" while their owners vacation, or their owners hire someone to stay overnight, so the dogs don't have to leave their comfortable home. Dogs now have their own private cemeteries with expensive tombstones.

Shep would never have let us dress him in doggie clothes. He had self-respect; he was a real dog, not a sissy dog. He took his baths in the farm creek. He had a real dog smell of the outdoors and farm, not of fancy, expensive soap and perfume.

While millions of dollars are being spent on dogs, missionaries struggle to raise support to go to the field where God wants them; pastors and church staff go underpaid;. ministry outreaches and programs lack support; children starve for lack of food; people die from lack of medical care; the homeless go hungry and continue to live in cardboard shelters; and the lost never hear the great news of the gospel message. How sad. Where are our priorities, our values? It truly can be said, "Our culture has gone to the dogs." Do you waste your God-given financial resources on your pets?

Memory is the treasure house of things we put in it, and even today I treasure the memories of my faithful companion, Shep.

> A beautiful collie dog was Ol' Shep;
> Full of love, life, and pep.
> He loved people, and he loved trains;
> But from chasing them he would not refrain.
> Then one day early in spring,
> He did a very foolish thing.
> Of a speeding train he had no fear;
> With a bound and leap, he got too near.
> He approached the train with a rush;
> We found his body in the brush.
> Ol' Shep was near age eleven;
> Now he is in doggie heaven.
> —*Author*

WAKARUSA (BETHLEHEM)

"Saturday Night in a Small, Country Town"

But as for you, Bethlehem Ephrathah, too little to be among the clans of Judah, from you One will go forth for Me to be ruler in Israel. His goings forth are from long ago, from the days of eternity.

Micah 5:2 (NAS)

"Boys, it is time to stop playing and get the chores done. It will soon be time to go to town," Mother called.

The ball game ended abruptly. With growing anticipation, we ran to the barn to start the chores. How we—my brothers, sister, and I—looked forward to going to our country town! In our eagerness, not all the milk was drained (squeezed) out of our one milk cow, the horses got less corn and hay, and the hogs got a little less slop. We were anxious to get going!

When the chores and care of the livestock were completed, we took our weekly baths, ate a hurried supper, and piled into our 1939 Dodge car. What an expectation we had for our Saturday night trip to town. It would be great fun after a week of farm work and school.

Small, country towns have a uniqueness and flavor all their own. Wakarusa (Indian name meaning "knee deep in mud" or "muddy") was no exception. From its friendly folks, variety of small, family-owned stores, restaurants and businesses, slow traffic and tree-lined streets to its one-and-only stoplight in the center of town, Wakarusa was truly a small, typical, rural town—a town where all the stores stayed open on Saturday night, even as late as midnight. Adding to its uniqueness at Christmastime was a large Christmas tree with a huge STAR on top, placed right in the center of Wakarusa's only downtown intersection, under the only traffic light, which prohibited left-hand turns by drivers from any direction for the season.

Situated in the heart of fertile farmland in northern Indiana, it was our family's hometown for many years. Of all the time spent there by us, Saturday nights were the best. Travel with me the four miles from our home, our farm, back into the past. Spend a carefree Saturday night with me in a rural, small town.

All week long Dad and Mom would make a list of things they needed from town. Although it was only four miles from the farm to town, we usually made the trip only once a week. During the Great Depression (1930s) and World War II (1940s), money and gas were very scarce. Thus, we only went to town when absolutely necessary. How different today. Now we drive four miles for a loaf of bread, and tomorrow we drive to the same store for a gallon of milk. I think our human "organizers" are broken down.

Dad would go to the only farm equipment dealer to buy parts for his machinery, tractors, combines, etc. Then it was off to the hardware store for smaller supplies, such as nails, bolts, fencing materials, and small tools. Then it was on to the barbershop where Dad and other local farmers gathered to discuss the weather, crops, farm prices, the war, the government, and much more. The barbershop was very large and could hold twenty to twenty-five people. Many who came were there only for the spirited discussions. It seemed to me, as a boy, these farmers knew how to solve all the local and world problems. They surely were a smart group that gathered at the barbershop!

How we kids looked forward to the Saturday night movies in the town park during the summer. The small cost of the movie, projector, and screen rentals was borne by the town merchants. I suspect that it was not just to entertain us kids, but rather a plan to free parents from watching their children, who for the most part did not really want to shop with Mom and Dad. This resulted in parents having more freedom and time to relax as they shopped, providing more sales for the merchants.

Mom would give us a nickel, and then we had to decide whether we wanted a big bag of fresh homemade potato chips or a big bag of hot, buttered popcorn. The chips were so fresh, crunchy, and delicious. On the other hand, for a nickel we could get a big bag of buttered popcorn. Usually, we chose the popcorn because we knew Mom would often buy chips to take home. The popcorn stand was so unique; a local family would pull their colorful, circus-like popcorn wagon into the center of town. It was white with colorful stenciling, just large enough for two people, a big popper, a cash register, and room for supplies.

Once we had our popcorn or potato chips, we raced to the town park to see the movie. My favorites were westerns with Roy Rogers, Tom Mix, Gene Autry, or occasionally a John Wayne or

Jimmy Stewart movie. And, of course, there were the comedies with Abbott and Costello, Ma and Pa Kettle, and others. All of these movies were in black and white.

The projector or film would often break. However, we didn't mind; we just waited or played in the park. There were no seats; we sat on the ground in front of the screen. After all, we were tough farm kids—we didn't need chairs!

During the winter or rainy nights, they would not have the movies. We would help Mom shop, carry the bags of food to the car, and do whatever else was expected of us. Or, we would go with Dad to the barbershop and listen to the stories about crop yields (usually embellished).

When the movies were over and Mom had finished her shopping, we would pile into the car for the four-mile drive back home. As we traveled, we would coax Dad to go real "fast." Being the good Dad he was, he would accelerate to forty miles per hour. Wow! We were flying! Or so it seemed to a young boy. Mom would say, "Dad, slow down. You will cause us to wreck." However, her fussing at Dad seemed half-hearted. I think down deep she enjoyed our "wild" ride at the reckless speed of forty miles per hour.

As we fell asleep, we were happy because our movie heroes, the "good guys," had saved the day, and we had another great Saturday night in Wakarusa.

The years have flown by, and the Saturday nights in a small country town are mostly distant memories. However, they are briefly revived every time I read about Bethlehem in Scriptures. I begin to wonder what Saturday night in Bethlehem was like. What did Jesus and other boys do? I am sure there were no movies to

watch in the park, no popcorn stands. However, there were merchants and stores, and perhaps the men sat around telling stories of
the exodus from Egypt and the Red Sea miracle. Or, the story of
the great, God-given victories in conquering the Promised Land.
Perhaps they heard the stories of David's life as first a shepherd boy
and then king. I wonder if Jesus and the other children got as
excited about the story of David slaying that big giant, Goliath, as
I did when one of my cowboy heroes "whupped" the bad guys?
The stories (history) of Israel's victories and failures covering over
2,000 years would have made for a great Saturday night in a park
in Bethlehem.

In my mind's eye, I see the best storyteller in Bethlehem, with
the excited kids seated around him (or her), telling one of the great
stories of their ancestors' great, God-given victories.

Bethlehem, just six miles south of Jerusalem, was a place that
was small in size but mighty in its prominence in Israel's history.
Rachel was buried there (Genesis 35:19). Bethlehem is spoken of
seven times in the book of Ruth. It was the hometown of Naomi,
Boaz, and eventually home for Ruth. It was where Boaz and Ruth
were married and resided.

It was where David was born and anointed king. And the greatest honor of all was bestowed upon Bethlehem when Jesus, Savior
and Lord of all creation, including mankind, was born there.

Helena, the mother of Constantine, in AD 325 had a church
erected that remains to this day in Bethlehem. It was erected on
the site (as best determined) where Jesus was born. It is known as
the Church (or place) of Nativity.

Saturday night in a small country town, with a star at the top of a Christmas tree, was a special treat for a young boy. More important is the fact that the "Star of Bethlehem" shines in my heart and soul. Like the wise men of old, have you followed the Star of Bethlehem to find the Lord Jesus Christ?

BOUNTIFUL HARVEST

"The Wagons Are Running Over"

And He was saying, "The kingdom of God is like a man who casts seed upon the soil; and he goes to bed at night and gets up by day, and the seed sprouts and grows—how, he himself does not know. The soil produces crops by itself; first the blade, then the head, then the mature grain in the head. But when the crop permits, he immediately puts in the sickle, because the harvest has come."

Mark 4:26-29 (NAS)

One hundred fifty bushels per acre! There was a song in my heart and a smile on my face as I looked at the results of a measurement to determine the yield of a field of golden ripe, soon-to-be-harvested corn.

The planting and growing season had been just right. First, the ground was soft for planting. Then, there were timely rains. We were able to keep the field free of weeds. The temperatures were ideal for the growing and ripening of the grain. Wow! What a harvest it was going to be.

Now Dad and I were standing in the field, looking at the coming bountiful harvest. After a few minutes of silence, Dad turned to me and said, "Son, you may not know the passage of Mark 4:26-29, but it tells how this happened." He continued. "First, we prepared a proper seed bed; then, we planted the seed, and while we slept, the seed sprouted. The roots went down, and then after about ten days, we saw the first blade."

As Dad paused, I asked, "Dad, what caused the hard, lifeless seed to sprout?"

"Son, it is a miracle of creation, of God. He causes it to grow. As the Scriptures tell us, we don't know how or why a cold, hard, dry, seemingly dead seed, when exposed to water, air, and light, can germinate and grow."

Photosynthesis! It literally means "Put together with light." It is the most important process on earth. Without it, both man and animals (even fish and reptiles) would have nothing to eat. Soon all would die, first the plants and trees, then animals, and eventually, man. Without the photosynthesis process, plants would not manufacture the needed food and energy to sustain life. Animals eat plants to live. The carnivorous animals live and have their sustenance by feeding on plant-eating animals. And, of course, man eats both plants and animals, thus sustaining human life. Of all the creations of God, plants are the only living things that can produce their own food within themselves, thanks to the photosynthesis miracle.

It is well known that it takes three ingredients to start the photosynthesis process: light (energy), air (carbon), and water. These three ingredients then combine and produce food and energy for plant growth. Even today, scientists don't know exactly how the process of both germination and photosynthesis works. Is this what Jesus was referring to in Mark 4:27, ...man knows not how..."? I think so.

Now the results of the two miracles of both new growth and photosynthesis were evident. From the stalks hung ripe, full ears of corn, waiting to be harvested.

As we continued to gaze upon the results of God's bountiful blessing, Dad continued, "Son, do you remember the miracle of the feeding of the 5,000?" (Matthew 14:14-21; Mark 6:34-44; Luke 9:12-17; John 6:5-13)

"Yes, Dad, I do. However, I find it hard to believe that story. To take five loaves and two fish and feed 5,000 is a little beyond my understanding."

With an amused look, Dad said, "Why, Son, would you believe that miracle if you saw it happen today?"

"I sure would, Dad," I responded.

"Son, there is a similar miracle in front of you. What was one kernel is now full ears with 200 kernels. The half bushel of seed we planted on each acre is now 150 bushes." He paused and then winked at me. "The feeding of the 5,000 from five loaves and two fish took perhaps a few minutes, while the miracle of this increase took five months. But, nevertheless, it is still a miracle, brought about by God."

As the years have passed, I have often thought of that particular bountiful harvest and how it has so many spiritual applications.

When a baby is born, it is the seed of a man and woman, and the miracle of God's creation takes place.

When the seed of salvation falls upon the soft, receptive bed of the heart, the new birth takes place; a miracle of God. As a new Christian becomes rooted and grounded in God's Word, a bountiful harvest of spiritual fruit and more miracles takes place.

What a bountiful harvest of souls Peter and John had on the day of Pentecost (Acts 2).

When I read the biographies of Billy Sunday, Dwight Moody, Bob Jones Sr., and other evangelists, my heart cries out, "WOW! God has done it again." What a bountiful harvest of souls God gave to these men.

Daily, we as Christians should be spreading and teaching God's Word—spiritual seed—both by word and our daily walk. We do not know how, when, or in what manner God will give the increase of spiritual fruit. One thing I do know from what I learned in the cornfield is that God will, by His miracles of creation and increase, take the seeds and bring forth a bountiful, fruitful, spiritual harvest, and the miracles of increase continue. Dad and I prepared a good seed bed, planted the seed, and carefully cultivated, but it was God who gave the increase.

Are you sowing spiritual seed daily?

HOBOS

"Can You Spare Some Food?"

*Then the King will say to those on His right, "Come, you
who are blessed of my Father, inherit the kingdom prepared for
you from the foundation of the world. For I was hungry, and
you gave me something to eat; I was thirsty, and you gave me
something to drink; I was a stranger, and you invited me in;
naked and you clothed me; I was sick, and you visited me; I
was in prison, and you came to me."*

Matthew 25:34-36

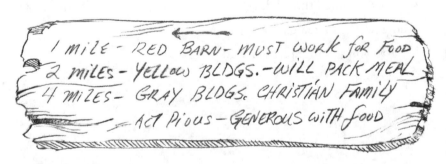

"Ma'am, could you spare some food for a hungry man?"
I had seen him slowly walking down the road
from the railroad toward our home as I played in our shady front
yard. Now he stood facing my mom. He was thin and had a

sad look in his eyes. His clothes were worn out, even tattered, but clean.

"Ma'am, if you could share some food with me, I would be most thankful."

To a five-year-old boy, he seemed so sad and lonely, as well as hungry. I was so touched by his soft but urgent request that I would have gladly shared my lunch with him.

The year was 1939. The great economic depression was still burdening our country. Thousands of men, desperate for work, often rode the empty boxcars on the railroad from city to city, looking for work. They were known as the "Railroad Hobos." They came from many former walks of life—from the blue collar factory worker to the top level executives. Now, hundreds of thousands of men were riding the rails in search of a job—any job.

My mom responded with a hearty, "We have plenty of food. You are welcome to share our noon meal, and I will also send a package of food with you."

With my mom's warm, loving response, the hobo's eyes brightened and sagging shoulders straightened. "Ma'am, I will be willing to work for the food. Is there anything I can do?"

My mother then proceeded to put the hobo to work cutting and splitting wood, which he cheerfully did until the noon meal was served.

Most men of that era were of such strong character that they wanted to work for their food. It was difficult for them to accept a free handout. Hunger is one of the most degrading of adversities. It demonstrates the inability of a person to furnish even the barest, most fundamental of life's necessities.

As we ate our noon meal, our visitor shared that back home he had a wife and four children. They were living with his parents, as he had lost both his job and home. As he shared his story, tears came to his eyes; he longed for his family.

The Great Depression was difficult for everyone. In the very early 1930's, my parents married. They bought a 160-acre farm, and in the next eight years Mom gave birth to four children. Times were tough. But, as I look back, I realize I was learning two great lessons: first, that God does always provide and is truly Jehovah-Jireh—the God who will provide for all our needs, all the time, everywhere; and second, that as God provides for our needs, He often provides enough to share with others. God had provided us with a large garden full of vegetables, an orchard full of fruit, and barns filled with fat livestock. Praise be to God!

When trains would stop in Wakarusa, the town four miles to the east of our farm, or in Wyatt, a town four miles to the west, the hobos would walk to our farm (and some other farms along the railroad) for a meal. For many years I wondered how the hobos knew where to find food. Then I learned that the hobos had a "Hobo Code" that directed hungry men to a warm meal and caring strangers. Both verbally and by signs usually posted at railroad stations or at a "Hobo Camp" on a tree or post (see the picture at the end of this chapter), they learned who in a community would be Christ-like in sharing God's blessings. The Bible is our "Hobo Code," so to speak. It directs us to where the best of spiritual food and heavenly feasting can be found. Along the road of life, Bible "food" can bring a fullness of satisfaction and contentment to the soul, peace and joy to the heart, and encouragement to the mind.

Recently, I had the privilege of reading a book titled We Had Everything but Money (Reminisce Books). It is a collection of human interest stories from the 1930's Great Depression. It made me remember how I learned, as a child from my parents' example, the biblical principle of sharing with those in need. People of that time, along with my parents, knew the story Jesus told about a Good Samaritan. There were hundreds of thousands of good Samaritans in the 1930's.

Currently, our country is in an economic recession. It is nothing compared to the thirty-five percent unemployment rate of the 1930's. Yet people today constantly complain and whine, even to the point of bitterness, because they can't afford to buy a new car as often as they would like, or they can't go out to a restaurant daily, or they can't buy as many new clothes, or they can't vacation as much. The list can go on and on. How ashamed we should be! Christians, especially, should be ashamed. Have we forgotten God's instruction found in I Timothy 6:6-8 (KJV)? "But godliness with contentment is great gain. For we brought nothing into this world, and it is certain we can carry nothing out. And having food and raiment, let us be therewith content." Or have we also forgotten the promise in Psalm 37:25 (KJV)? "I have been young, and now am old; yet have I not seen the righteous forsaken, nor his seed begging bread."

As pointed out often in the book, families, neighbors, and communities pulled together in love and sharing. As God provided a home, a vehicle, food, or clothing, it was shared with others.

Thanks be to parents who, at an early age, showed me how to share God's blessings with others. In the 1930s, as businesses and banks closed, hearts and homes opened up. Much of the entertainment of the time was listening to the radio. Families, friends, and neighbors would gather around a radio in a home and listen to their favorite radio program. For many, pocketbooks were empty, but hearts were full of gratitude.

Which are you? Are you a selfish, hoarding person who is ungrateful for God's blessings and fails to share them? Or are you a rejoicing person, willing to share what He provides?

PARTY LINE

"The Royal Telephone"

Seek the LORD while He may be found; Call upon Him while He is near.

Isaiah 55:6 (NAS)

R ing! Ring! Ring! Ring!
"Son, will you answer the phone? That was our ring. I am busy in the kitchen," my mother called to me.

I rose from the dining room table, where I was putting together a puzzle, and headed toward the wall where the telephone hung. "Hello. Yes, this is the Geyer residence. ... I will tell Dad the part he ordered for the tractor is here. Goodbye." The conversation was brief and to the point.

As I placed the receiver back on its cradle, I had no idea how much telephone equipment and usage would change in the next sixty years, and I had no understanding of the similarities of talking on a phone and calling upon God in prayer.

In the early 1900s, the telephone spread rapidly across the United States. Thousands of wooden poles were placed in the ground, and millions of miles of wire were strung and fastened to the poles.

The new-fangled invention called the telephone was soon in most houses, even in rural areas.

There were only a few private lines; most were party lines. The party lines could have as few as four or as many as ten to twelve users. Each user had a certain number of rings. On our party line there were eight customers, so there could be anywhere from one to eight rings. Our number was four rings.

The telephone was mounted on the wall and consisted of three major parts—a receiver that hung on the left side in a cradle; a crank on the right side to notify the operator we wanted to make a call; and in the center, a mouthpiece on a stem, into which we spoke.

Our rural area had its own privately-owned phone company—Klondike Telephone Company—which had about six hundred customers. In the center of our farming community was a building that housed the equipment to handle the calls. We had two female operators, Maude and Mabel, who took our requests and plugged the wires into the appropriate holes, whether the call was local or long distance. The standard joke was that Maude and Mabel knew more about the phone subscribers' business than God Himself. Since the lines were party lines, almost every line had its busybody who would listen in on the neighbors' calls. Sometimes when we called, the operator would say that line was busy, or there would be no answer at all.

Out of respect for other party line families, calls were (for the most part) kept to a minimum of verbiage. An example of this was when I would call my girlfriend. (Girlfriend answers her phone. I speak.) "This is Jim. We are having a special music group at church on Sunday night. Would you come with me?" (Hopefully, there would be a "yes".) "Great. I will pick you up at 6:30. See you then. Goodbye." Since at least one parent was nearby and it was a party line, any romantic talk was kept for a later time.

Sometimes when we knew there was serious illness or near-death in our party line "family," Mom would listen in on their call. Then we could help and comfort a family even before their need was publicly made known.

The growing popularity and usage of the telephone led song-writers to spiritualize the telephone by writing hymns sung by millions of church-goers for many years. An example of this is the song called "The Royal Telephone" (see song at end of chapter). With the invention of the telephone, hundreds of thousands of Christians had a visible, tangible device that reminded them of how, through prayer, we talk to God, and through His Word and the Holy Spirit, He talks to us.

The Bible is replete with examples of people, especially the Old Testament prophets, calling God. Their calls were not only for instruction, but also for deliverance from both personal problems and physical enemies.

Noah may have been the first person to use a "cellular, mobile phone." I am sure that—after many months of floating in the ark with twenty-four-hour close proximity to both animals and family—he called God often for relief.

The prophets continually called God on the "Royal Telephone" to get instructions on what to say to the nation of Israel to warn them about coming judgment.

Daniel, we are told, talked to God at least three times a day (Daniel 6:10).

Jesus, before His betrayal, spent time on the "phone" talking to His Father. The only time God didn't answer His "phone" was when Jesus called from the Cross, "...My God, my God, why hast thou forsaken me?" (Matthew 27:46, KJV)

In today's culture, the phone has developed so that a user can not only talk to others, but can also get a weather forecast, find out how a favorite sports team is doing, send text messages, take and send pictures, and much more.

The mobile phone has become so widely used (and abused) that some users spend over fifty percent of their time on a phone, and States are passing laws against cell phone usage while driving.

What follows is a parody of my thoughts after recently seeing a cell phone user.

CELL PHONE CONSUMPTION

The cellular (cell) phone was to her ear as she stepped out of her car and walked across the parking lot. The phone was still to her ear as she entered the garden center. With her shoulder slightly lifted and her head cocked, she proceeded to select plants and place them in her shopping cart, all the while still talking on her cell phone.

Fifteen minutes later she approached the cashier with her phone still between her shoulder and ear. Still talking, she swiped her credit card, signed the screen, and with her free hand stuffed the receipt in her purse. Never a word was spoken to the cashier or anyone else. Still talking on her cell phone, she placed her plant purchases in her car. As she pulled out of the parking lot, she was still talking on her phone. She never spoke a single word to anyone during her visit.

Her performance on the cell phone left me utterly amazed. What a powerful shoulder she must have to continually hold her phone. I know she must be married to a chiropractor, for surely she would need her neck "cracked" and straightened every evening. It has to be uncomfortable at night as she sleeps with that phone still cradled to her ear. Her life must be totally consumed by the cell phone.

As she disappeared into traffic, I asked myself how we could have accomplished so much in this country without cell phones. We invented the automobile, won two world wars, developed atomic power, invented and developed airplanes, even jet planes, built thousands of miles of railroads, built the Golden Gate Bridge, Route 66, put space vehicles into orbit, put men on the moon, built the first computer, made outstanding medical advances—all done without a single cell phone. AMAZING! All of those accomplishments without the use of a single cell phone.

As I think about the future of this country and cell phones, I can see at least five things happening:

First, medical schools will offer courses on how to surgically remove a cell phone from a person's shoulder and ear. Without a doubt, some people will hold a phone between their shoulder and ear so long that skin will cover the phone, bonding shoulder and ear together.

Second, clothing manufacturers will need to make blouses, shirts, and dresses a little longer on the shoulder side that holds the phone.

Third, there will need to be special counseling services set up for husbands (or wives) and children who have been "orphaned" by the cell phone or parents "orphaned" by children.

Fourth, the phone companies will want monuments in the shape of a large cell phone placed in every state where we can come and worship at its base.

Fifth, it would not surprise me if Congress changes the historical meaning of B.C. - Before Christ to B.C. - Before Cell phones.

If you agree with, or have enjoyed this brief exposé, please call me on your—you guessed it—cell phone.

Also, voice mail has become all too common a part of our everyday lives. The following is a parody of voice mail:

Most of us have learned to live with voice mail as a necessary part of our lives. Have you ever wondered what it would be like if God decided to install voice mail?

Imagine praying and hearing the following:

★ - Thank you for calling heaven.
    For English - Press 1
    For Spanish - Press 2
    For all other languages - Press 3
★ - Please select one of the following options:
    For Requests - Press 1
    For Thanksgiving - Press 2
    For Complaints - Press 3
    For All Others - Press 4

★ - I am sorry, all of our angels and saints are busy helping other sinners right now.

However, your prayer is important to us, and we will answer it in the order it was received. Please stay on the line.

★ - If you would like to speak directly to:

God - Press 1

Jesus - Press 2

Holy Spirit - Press 3

★ - To find a loved one who has been assigned to heaven, Press 5, then enter the person's Social Security number, followed by the pound sign.

★ - For reservations to heaven, please enter J-O-H-N followed by the numbers 3, 16.

★ - For answers to nagging questions about dinosaurs, life, and other planets, please wait until you arrive in heaven for the specifics.

★ - Our computers show that you have already been prayed for today. Please hang up and call again tomorrow.

★ - The office is now closed for the weekend and to observe a religious holiday.

★ - If you are calling after hours and need emergency assistance, please contact your local pastor.

★ - Thank you and have a heavenly day.

—*Author Unknown*

Praise be to God, we have direct access to Him through the Holy Spirit. Unlike the party line, God's "line" is never busy. Praise be to God who is always there to answer our call. Unless we are praying publicly, only He knows of our needs, fears, concerns, etc. There is no busybody to overhear our call and gossip about our needs and desires.

Certainly God is always calling us through His Word and Spirit. Sadly, we often don't answer when God calls.

The telephone, with all of its latest technological advances, is a marvelous invention. It certainly is an expedient way to take care of business, and the mobile phone is a great thing in case of emergency.

Sadly, like so many good inventions that God has given us, we have abused it to a point where we spend more time talking to others than to God, and more time listening to others than listening to God.

Do you answer when He calls? Do you spend more time on the phone talking to others than talking to God?

SUPPERTIME

"A TIME OF FUN, FOOD, AND FELLOWSHIP"

Then they made Him a supper. . .

John 12:2 (KJV)

"Suppertime! Please don't use that word. I don't like it." With that said, he walked away.

This sharp, quick, negative response had come from a colleague at work after I said to him that I was leaving because it was suppertime. I wanted to yell after him as he walked away that supper is a wonderful, biblical word; a word that should evoke pleasant memories of good food, sharing, and fellowship with family and friends. Perhaps the word "supper" brought back unpleasant memories of his childhood. He did not share the reason for his dislike; he just walked away.

In our modern-day culture, supper is a word seldom used. The three main meals used to be breakfast (morning), dinner (noon), and supper (evening). As society moved from one of much physical activity and manual labor to one of very little physical exertion, such as sitting behind a desk viewing a computer, less food was required to maintain energy levels. The meals became breakfast, lunch (noon), and dinner (evening). As the transition took place and supper was dropped from our vocabulary, we lost the true meaning of what an evening meal should be and its importance to a family.

I have many precious, pleasant memories about suppertime as I grew up. Mom was insistent that we eat at 6:00 p.m. every day. So Dad, my two brothers, and I would hurry to complete the evening chores of feeding the livestock to make the 6:00 deadline. Sometimes we finished the chores early enough to get in a game of good "Hoosier" barn basketball, always knowing that a great supper awaited us.

Soon we were seated as a family at a table of deliciously prepared, home-grown food (no KFC in the good old days), as only my sister Arlene and Mom could prepare. As the meal progressed, we shared the activities of the day and our thoughts: what had happened in school that day; what did we learn; would it snow enough during the night that school would be canceled; would our basketball team win the big game coming up against arch-rival Wakarusa; how many fish Uncle Warren had caught; what we would like for Christmas; could we stay at Grandpa and Grandma's house for three days next summer; World War II: were we winning and when would it end; was Franklin Roosevelt or Harry Truman a really good president; could we go to the big, big town of South Bend and shop at Sears (we boys needed new fishing tackle); and could we go to the bookstore so I could buy the latest Zane Gray book?

Not only was there a time of sharing and relationship-building around the table, it was a time when Dad and Mom were building in us principles of integrity, morality, and a love for God, His Word, and creation.

After the meal was finished, Dad would turn on the radio. As Mom and Arlene cleared the table and washed dishes, we all listened to the Lone Ranger. (In today's society, we "men" would be called "male chauvinists" for letting the women do all the work.) In our mind's eye, we rode with the Lone Ranger (and Tonto) over mountains, plains, and deserts as he whipped the "bad guys." What a great program it was to learn that good can triumph over evil, regardless of the circumstances and adversities. How different it is today, as the immoral person is often the hero.

After supper we spent the rest of the evening in study, reading, and playing games. I believe it was relationships at supper that built the strong family bond that we, as sister and brothers, enjoy yet today.

In today's culture, because our various work, school, and athletic activities have become our top priority, we eat "on the run," a fast meal at a fast food place, in the car or in front of the TV. What should be, at minimum, a half-hour meal becomes a five-minute "gulp." Thank goodness some families still make suppertime a top priority.

For a period of time, my wife and I ate in front of the TV, watching the evening news. Recently, we went back to eating supper at the kitchen table. We discovered that our level of sharing, communicating the day's events, God's blessings, concerns, and future planning improved and increased considerably.

Supper is a descriptive word meaning not only a good meal, but a time when sharing, fellowship, and positive relationships are formed. The word "supper" or "sup" is used seventeen times in

God's Word, and most of the references deal with a time of food and fellowship.

    ★   The importance of supper not just to family and friends, but also to the poor (Luke 14:12-14).

    ★   The cost of being indifferent to the supper that God has prepared (Luke 14:15-24).

    ★   The honor that the Lord can receive at supper as Mary poured out her adoration of the Lord (John 12:1-8).

    ★   The last meal Christ had with His disciples was the Passover supper (not breakfast or dinner [John 13:1-4]).

    ★   Sacred communion is known as the Lord's Supper (I Corinthians 11:20-34).

    ★   Culminating in the grand and glorious Marriage Supper when the church, the saints, are wed to Christ (Revelation 19:9).

Within the past year, several articles have appeared about the importance of the family eating together. In an article titled "Families who eat together bring multiple benefits to and from the table," the author quotes statistics from the National Center on Addiction and Substance Abuse (CASA). The facts show that families who share meals together have healthier children who do better in school and are much less likely to use and abuse drugs, alcohol, and tobacco.

Family meals and the communication that occurs over the course of a meal are critical in building relationships with your children and helping them understand the world culture in which they live.

SUPPER! A family gathering for supper is a miniature picture; a microcosm of the great Marriage Supper when we will as

Christians gather around God's table of heavenly blessings of joy, peace, praise, sharing, singing, fellowship, and all kinds of spiritual food. Soon the earthly "chores" will be over, and we will gather for God's eternal supper. Mom and Dad, is suppertime a priority at your house?

COON HUNTING

"Barking Up the Wrong Tree"

"Many will say to me in that day, Lord, Lord, have we not prophesied in thy name? and in thy name have cast out devils? and in thy name done many wonderful works? And then will I profess unto them, I never knew you: depart from me, ye that work iniquity."

Matthew 7:22-23 (KJV)

"Jim, can I bring my new coon (raccoon) dog out to your farm tonight? I want to try him and see if he can really track a coon, and I want you to go with me."

It was my friend, Red, owner of many coon dogs, who was calling me. He loved his dogs and was an avid hunter. I hesitated in answering. I could only think of tracking through fields, woodlands, and marshes at night. Did I really want to follow some unproven dog, chasing after a yet-to-be-found coon? Sensing my uncertainty, Red said, "This new coon dog has a very sweet howl when it's on the trail. You will like the sound."

"OK, Red, I will go. I will see you at seven o'clock."

At the appointed hour, Red arrived in his old, weathered pickup truck. From the back he opened one of the cage doors, and out came an ordinary-looking hound dog.

"What do you think of this beauty?" Red asked.

"Well, Red, he looks like a normal coon dog," I said.

"Wait 'til you hear his 'sweet song' on the trail," Red responded, a little irritated that I had not made a bigger fuss over his new purchase.

After a few minutes of preparation, including making sure our flashlights worked, we headed out to test Red's new coon dog.

It was a cold, wet November night. It had rained earlier in the day, and now the cold dampness seemed to penetrate our warm clothing. It was an ideal night for coons to be out hunting food, but a dismal night for humans.

We headed for the creek where I knew coons came to drink. In a few minutes the dog picked up the scent of a coon and began a melodic "I found the trail" barking. I must admit, it was a good-sounding dog Red had purchased.

The coon's trail led across the creek, where the water was a little deeper than our boots. Already our socks were wet and our feet cold.

Then, across the harvested cornfield we went, stumbling over the corn stalks and even sprawling headlong in the mud on two occasions.

Soon we came to the edge of a large woods. The coon's trail led into the woods, and as we followed, we were quickly at the mercy of briars, brambles, and brush, all seemingly hitting and scratching us from all sides. Then the coon decided to take the dog and us through a marshy area. The dismal mud sucked at our boots, making every step an exercise in perseverance. I could not believe I had agreed to help Red try out his new dog.

I was cold, wet, bleeding from scratches, and now I was in the middle of a swamp in darkness (with the exception of two flashlights), trying to reach some sort of solid ground and not even knowing if the dog was really chasing a coon or just an old coon trail.

"Hear that?" Red exclaimed. "He has treed a coon!"

Just ahead of us we could hear the excited bark of the dog, indicating the coon was in a tree. In the middle of the swamp was some higher ground, upon which stood two trees. We came to where the dog was circling the tree with tail furiously wagging and frantic barking. We pointed our lights into the tree and found it to be empty. Empty! No coon! How can this be?

I was about to kill the dog for leading us on a two-hour fruitless, miserable chase.

"Wait a minute," Red muttered, "let's flash our lights in the other tree."

And there he was, a big coon sitting on one of the branches, seeming to gloat in the fact that he had led us on an exhausting and miserable chase. Apparently, the coon had circled the first tree and then ran over to climb the second tree, and of course it had fooled Red's new dog.

There are forty references in Scripture about dogs, and most of them have a negative connotation. As we stood— wet, cold, and scratched—looking at the coon, I had a very negative attitude about both the dog and the coon.

"Red, let's not shoot the coon and then have to carry it all the way home. Its pelt is not worth that much, and you have found out your dog can trail pretty good," I said with exhaustion in my voice. He agreed, and with that, we headed back home to dry clothing and a warm house.

During my lifetime I have come to the realization that many people are "barking up the wrong tree" when it comes to salvation and going to heaven.

The well-dressed man I was witnessing to seemed sincere enough when it came to wanting to go to heaven, but when it came to salvation, I found he was trusting in his denomination to get to heaven. God used many great reformers, e.g., Luther, Knox, and Calvin, in the fifteenth, sixteenth and seventeenth centuries to snatch His true church from the clutches of the corrupt Roman Catholic church.

But over a period of time, men began to worship a denomination— Lutheran, Presbyterian, Baptist, etc.—rather than a diety, the Lord Jesus Christ. How tragic when man depends upon a denomination to be eternally saved. Jesus said in John 14:6 (KJV), "I am the way, the truth, and the life: no man cometh unto the Father, but by me."

For those who are looking for their denomination to save them—sorry, but you are "barking up the wrong tree".

He was a true philanthropist. He had given over a million dollars to a very worthy cause. In a subsequent newspaper interview, it was painfully obvious he was trying to buy his way into heaven. Along with many millions of others, he believed his money could buy his way into an eternal paradise. Philanthropy is in itself a good thing. The money given by well-meaning people has financially helped many worthwhile organizations. Philanthropy has fed the hungry, clothed the naked, and put a roof over the homeless.

Philanthropy is a great thing, but it won't buy heaven. Simon the sorcerer tried to buy both heaven and the power of the Holy Spirit. He failed (Acts 8:9-25). The parable of the rich man and the beggar, Lazarus, (Luke 16:19-31) illustrates clearly that money can't buy heaven. In the passage of Scripture found in John 3:1-7 (KJV)—the story of Nicodemus seeking salvation—Jesus makes it clear and simple: "Ye must be born again" (vs. 7). Born again by the living Holy Spirit in order to "see the kingdom of God" (vs. 3). Jesus said in John 8:12 (KJV), "I am the light of the world: he that followeth me shall not walk in darkness, but shall have the light of life."

Since the beginning of time, many have sought to buy heaven, but one day God will say to them, "Sorry, you have been barking up the wrong tree."

"As a pioneer, my great-grandfather helped settle his community in which he lived. He gave land for a church to be built, and he helped build it with his time and money," the young man said. As we sat discussing spiritual things, it soon became evident he was trusting in his ancestors' salvation for his own. Salvation is a personal thing. Nowhere in Scripture can one find any reference to one's family bringing personal redemption. When Nicodemus came to Jesus, He said, "You (personal) must be born again." Jesus made it clear in John 11:25 (KJV): "I am the resurrection, and the life: he that believeth in me, though he were dead, yet shall he live."

Notice the three personal pronouns (he) used in this verse. No family heritage salvation is found in this verse or any others.

Those who are depending upon godly ancestors for salvation—sorry, you are "barking up the wrong tree."

"I know all my volunteer work will get me into heaven," she exclaimed. "For over twenty-five years I have spent hundreds of hours taking food to the poor. I have visited many sick people in the hospital, and . . ." and her list of good works went on and on. Christians should do good works, as commanded by Christ. But, our salvation is in Christ, not our works. Paul clearly states, in Ephesians 2:8-9 (KJV) that "For by grace are ye saved through faith; and that not of yourselves: it is the gift of God: Not of works, lest any man should boast."

For those who are depending upon their good works for eternal salvation—sorry, the Bible clearly states you are "barking up the wrong tree."

"I know God will look favorably upon me, because I am study-ing for the ministry." Sincerely, the young man believed his study and eventual ministry work would be his salvation. "After all," he argued, "I will be helping others. I will be a shepherd to those who need help." Not once in our conversation did he mention biblical instruction and counseling as a shepherd. His approach to helping others would be humanistic.

Doctors, nurses, health care workers, teachers, policemen, fire-men, etc. have openly shared with me that their noble profession was their ticket to heaven. How sad. Although they have and would help many, even saving lives in the future, and in some cases even willing to give their lives as shepherds to fulfill their life's mission, they still didn't know the true Shepherd. Jesus tells us in John 10:11 (KJV), "I am the good shepherd: the good shepherd giveth his life for the sheep." Sheep that know not the true Shepherd are "barking up the wrong tree."

"Based upon my feelings, I know I am going to heaven," she proudly stated.

"Emotions are fickle," I countered. "Salvation is based upon God's promise, not our emotions," I explained. From God's Word with such passages as John 3:16, 36 and Romans 10:9-10, I shared that God's promises are our assurance of eternal salvation and not how we feel at the moment. If salvation depended upon our feelings, many would be lost every morning before their first cup of coffee.

Sadly, churches, pastors, and others lead their people to believe that the right feelings are salvation. Salvation, for many, is how well they can speak in tongues, how loudly they can shout an "amen," or how long and loudly they pray. Jesus stated in John 6:35 (KJV), "I am the bread of life: he that cometh to me shall never hunger; and he that believeth on me shall never thirst."

Salvation should bring about great emotions, not the reverse. Feeding upon the "bread" of the Word will bring about a true satisfaction with no hungering or thirsting for eternal salvation. Passages like John 3:16-18 and 36 are just a few of the Scriptures that make it crystal clear: salvation is a fact, not an emotion.

If you are depending upon your emotions or just good feelings to get you to heaven, you are "barking up the wrong tree."

"My education, my knowledge, has shown me there is no heaven or hell," he informed me as I discovered he had two masters degrees and an earned doctorate. "My learning of the 'truth' has led me to believe there is no life after death. In my studies I have found no evidence of any future life," he proclaimed. He was a true fulfillment of 2 Timothy 3:7 (KJV), "Ever learning, and never able to come to the knowledge of the truth."

Solomon, in his wisdom, tells us knowledge is not supreme. Ecclesiastes 12:12-13 (KJV) states, "And further, by these, my son, be admonished: of making many books there is no end; and much study is a weariness of the flesh. Let us hear the conclusion of the whole matter: Fear God, and keep his commandments: for this is the whole duty of man."

If anyone's education would be a requirement for, or way to, heaven, it was the Apostle Paul's. A blinding light, a voice from heaven, and Paul realized it was not education that really mattered. It was knowing Jesus. As Jesus states, the door to heaven is unlocked and opened not by education, but by Jesus Himself —John 10:9 (KJV): "I am the door: by me if any man enter in, he shall be saved, and shall go in and out, and find pasture."

We are biblically commanded to learn, to grow in knowledge and wisdom as found in the Proverbs and as stated in II Timothy 2:15 (KJV), "Study to shew thyself approved unto God, a workman that needeth not to be ashamed, rightly dividing the word of truth." But, that in itself is not salvation.

I have news for those who are depending upon their education to gain salvation. You are "barking up the wrong tree."

On that cold, miserable night in the middle of a swamp, did I know how many people I would meet and to whom I would witness concerning salvation, who would be just like Red's new coon dog, "barking up the wrong tree"? No, I didn't. The experience of that night has surely helped me understand how easily people can be misled about salvation. Up which tree are you barking? The false tree, or the only true Tree of Life—Jesus Christ, Lord and Savior?

LOST RELATIONSHIPS

"Roadside Friendships"

Carry each other's burdens, and in this way you will fulfill the law of Christ.

Galatians 6:2

Recently, as I filled my vehicle with gas at a local gas station, I used my debit card to pay at the pump. During this time I spoke to no one. As I slipped behind the steering wheel, I paused and reflected for a moment about how, in today's society, we have lost something very important—personal relationships. Yes, I had saved a few minutes by paying at the pump, but I had lost a chance to build a relationship with someone, perhaps someone who needed to hear a cheerful word of encouragement or just see a friendly, smiling face.

As I drove away from the gas station, I reflected upon how rich my life had been when I lived in a country community where greeting my neighbors or those with whom I did business was a daily occurrence. Even today, the memories of those relationships established are so sweet and refreshing. Let me share a few memories with you.

Oftentimes as I drove along the country roads, I would stop the vehicle I was driving—car, truck, or tractor—and fellowship for at least a few minutes with a neighbor. We would discuss anything—weather, crops, markets, or our kids. Many times, it was a word of encouragement or a question of "how can I help you?" A few of the relationships that were made then, still exist today. Certainly, the memories of those relationships formed bring a pleasure beyond measure, many years later.

My memories include the relationships created at the local gas station. The owner knew his customers by their first names. He knew their families and their needs. He greeted his customers with an enthusiastic "hello" or "good morning," and usually followed with "how can I help you or your family?" His was not just a gas station—it was a "caring" station. His station became a local gathering place for the nearby farmers, a place where the neighbors could embellish their crop yields or the power of their tractors. But, more importantly, it was a place where one could share needs, concerns, and yes, even one's hopes and dreams. The local gas station was a place where lasting relationships were nurtured and built.

My memories include the relationships developed with the owners of the local feed and grain elevators, or food and clothing merchants in a small, country town; a time and place where the merchants knew their customers by their needs and endeavored not just to make money but to form long-time relationships of trust and friendship.

Shortly after I left the gas station, I went to a local bank's ATM. I wonder if ATMs have names? (I have called a few of them names.) They just don't seem to care how I feel. Their printed greeting on a screen consists mostly of written instructions that seem cold and heartless. And, if you don't push the correct buttons in sequence, it won't even give you your own money. What a difference between that machine and the friendly banker I once knew. He cared about me and my family, and he even had time to visit our home, on occasion. I have found it very difficult to build lasting relationships with machines.

The Bible is replete with examples of lasting friendships and relationships. Adam and Eve had the first and only perfect relationship, until they sinned. They walked and talked with God each evening. As they fellowshipped, they walked upon perfect soil and among perfect blooming plants and majestic trees. They petted the perfect animals and listened to the melodic singing of the perfect birds. "Adam, you did a great job of naming the animals," God could have said. "And the names of the plants and birds are just perfect." What a paradise in which to build a lasting, perfect relationship. And then its perfection came to an abrupt end.

In spite of the fact that there can be no perfect relationship built since man's Fall, examples of many strong relationships can be found in Scripture, such as Abraham and his servant Eliezer (Genesis 12-24). This long-lasting relationship had some very key ingredients that made for a rich, deep bond. Eliezer was consistent in being trustworthy, diligent, prayerful, honest, and discreet. Abraham treated and trusted him like a son, not a servant. The relationship was so pure and deep that Abraham trusted Eliezer to find a wife for Isaac.

Although Scripture gives no specifics, I believe there was a strong relationship between Joshua and Caleb. Certainly, there was a beautiful relationship between Naomi and Ruth. How often they must have shared each other's concerns, burdens, and hopes.

How often have we read or heard about the great relationship between David and Jonathan—one that was so deep that Jonathan risked his life for David and loved David more than himself (I Samuel 20)?

The Gospels record the eternal relationship between Christ and eleven of His disciples. So strong was the relationship built that eventually ten of the eleven gave their lives prematurely for Christ. In turn, Christ gave them eternal life.

Paul built lasting bonds of relationship with Silas, Barnabas, and Timothy. The strength of these relationships sent the glorious gospel to the "uttermost parts of the world."

The book of Proverbs eloquently teaches us how to build lasting relationships, and with whom.

The strong bond of friendship and relationship between George Washington and Henry Lee (father of Robert E. Lee) greatly helped in the Revolutionary War battles and the founding of our country.

Dad and Mom strongly emphasized the need to develop strong relationships, both by example and word. By their honesty and integrity, they developed lasting relationships with neighbors, fellow church members, and community merchants. Mom often said, "Son, your word is your bond. If you want to build lasting friendships and relationships, you must always remember that the building blocks are honesty, integrity, and high moral character. If you have a reputation of being immoral and dishonest, no one will want to be your friend or to do business with you."

When I was an educational consultant, I was often asked by school administrators, pastors, and parents about the best way to build their ministry. I would answer, "First build a strong relationship with God, then with each other and the community." I then further shared, "Development and marketing, such as ministry building, can be summed up in two words: Building Relationships."

Now, we have the computer and e-mail. These are marvelous, modern, high-tech (and sometimes frustrating) creations. However, from e-mails it is difficult to tell, unless they specifically write it, whether a person is glad, sad, happy, discouraged, angry, melancholy, etc. It was from those facial expressions, the body language, the voice inflections, that I learned about my neighbors and whether they were in need of any help. Certainly, relationships can be built by e-mail or letter, but only to a point. Relationships can only be fully developed when you put your arm around a neighbor, a friend, or even a customer and say, "How may I help you?"

My paying at the gas pump and my visit to an ATM machine sparked the memories of a time when strong relationships with families, friends, neighbors, and merchants were developed upon daily, personal interaction.

Advanced technology. Is it a blessing or a curse? Certainly it is a blessing in some ways. But, it is also a curse of our culture in the way it prevents the wonderful opportunity to create lasting personal relationships.

Our "now" generation has gained immediacy and convenience but has lost the wonderful opportunity to form lasting relationships with merchants, neighbors, and others. Please don't e-mail or text message me. Call me, or better yet, come by for a cup of coffee or tea, and we will build a relationship. How is your relationship building?

"No one should ever go on a journey (through life) with any other than him with whom one can walk arm in arm, in the evening, in the twilight, and agree that if either should have a son, he shall be named after the other." — Robert Cortes Holliday

DINNER BELL

"Sit Up and Pay Attention"

Cause me to hear thy lovingkindness in the morning; for in thee do I trust: cause me to know the way wherein I should walk; for I lift up my soul unto thee.

Psalm 143:8 (KJV)

Clang! Clang! Clang! Dad stopped the big horses pulling the plow and looked toward the house. "It is dinnertime. I will finish this round, and then we will go to the house to eat."

That sounded great to a seven-year-old boy who was always hungry for Mom's home-cooked meals. The sound we had heard was from the big, old dinner bell; it was an ordinary, rusty, forty-pound bell mounted on a wooden post just outside the back door of our house.

It was a warm, lazy spring day. In the morning, Dad had hitched our work horses, Bob and Sam (all horses were given names), to a riding plow. As Dad explained, it was going to be a great day to plow one of the fields to get it ready to plant corn.

After playing around the yard and barn for a few hours, I went to the field where Dad was plowing. I followed along in the eight-inch deep furrow behind the plow. It was fun to smell the newly-turned soil, see the squiggly earthworms, and watch the robins following us to feast on the worms.

Now Mom was calling us for dinner. Dad winked at me and said, "We will make one more round before we go to eat. Your mom always rings the bell early because she knows I will make one more round."

Most farms had a dinner bell, forerunner of the CB and then the cell phone. It was used not only to call us for a meal, but also to get our attention. If Mom had an urgent message, she would furiously ring the bell, and we would respond hurriedly by going to the house; it was sometimes used to warn us of a fire at a neighbor's building or in a field. How long and loud the bell was rung was an indication of the urgency.

I vividly remember how a passing steam engine on the railroad that ran along the edge of our farm had belched out hot cinders from its smokestack; a burning cinder started the grass and weeds on fire. It was quickly spreading into a dry wheat field ready for harvest. The dead stalks holding the ripened grain were about to become twenty acres of a hellish inferno, destroying thousands of dollars of grain. When Dad spotted the smoke, he yelled, "Mom, ring the bell and let the neighbors know there is an emergency—a fire." Quickly we grabbed shovels and burlap sacks and piled into the pickup truck, racing to the scene.

With a repeated frenzy, the bell was rung, alerting the neighbors. Soon they were flying down the road to the railroad tracks. With wet burlap sacks and shovels, they ran to the fire to join us in putting out the hot, scorching flames.

Soon the fire was extinguished, with only a small loss of grain. With blackened faces and hands, we thanked the neighbors and returned to the house for a glass of cool, refreshing lemonade.

As the dinner bell was used to get our attention, God uses various ways and methods to get our attention. It may be a serious illness of oneself or a family member; it may be an accident resulting in serious injury; or maybe even the death of a loved one. It could be the loss of a job or steady income. It may even be just a morning sunrise, evening sunset, a stroll through a flowery field, or a towering forest.

Perhaps God has gotten our attention through the reading or teaching of His Word. I love the way God used Samson to get the attention of the Philistines. In Judges 15:1-8, there is the account of how the Philistines had ignored Samson, even to the point of giving away his wife to another man. He got their attention by tying burning sticks to the tails of 300 foxes; he then released the foxes into their wheat fields, thus burning and destroying all the grain. (There were no smoking steam engines in those days!)

God got Moses' attention with a bush that was burning yet not consumed, and the Pharaoh's attention with the ten plagues (Exodus). The Angel of the Lord got Balaam's attention by standing in the way of his donkey. (The donkey had more spiritual insight than Balaam. [Numbers 22]) God got the "world's" attention with midday total darkness, earthquakes, and the rending of the huge temple veil when His Son died (Matthew 27). God got Paul's attention with a blinding light (heavenly lightning) and blindness (Acts 9).

Often we have heard our parents and teachers say "sit up and pay attention" when our minds and spirits were wandering. When our hearts and minds wander away from God, He says, "Sit up and pay attention." Then He uses some method to get our attention.

The old farm dinner bell was the method used to communicate many a message and get our attention. God uses many ways and methods to communicate His message to us. Are we listening?

For God does speak—now one way, now another—though man may not perceive it. In a dream, in a vision of the night, when deep sleep falls on men as they slumber in their beds, he may speak in their ears and terrify them with warnings, to turn man from wrongdoing and keep him from pride, to preserve his soul from the pit, his life from perishing by the sword.

Job 33:14-18

THE CATTLE ARE OUT

"THE FENCES ARE BROKEN DOWN"

They said to me, "Those who survived in the exile and are back in the province are in great trouble and disgrace. The wall of Jerusalem is broken down, and its gates have been burned with fire." When I heard these things, I sat down and wept. For some days I mourned and fasted and prayed before the God of heaven.

Nehemiah 1:3-4

The pounding of hooves on our driveway awakened me from my Sunday afternoon nap. It sent a cold chill up and down my spine. I knew immediately what had happened. The cattle had broken down the fence that held them in the feedlot. And now they were scattering rapidly into the lawn and garden and were headed for the cornfields and our neighbor's fields.

"Come quickly!" I yelled to the family. "We must round up the cows before they do untold damage to the garden, cornfields, and neighbor's crops!"

Neighbors were called, and the roundup began. After several months of being confined, the cattle seemingly went wild at their newfound freedom. They ran in circles around the yard and garden. They pawed the ground, throwing dirt into the air. They went into the cornfields, knocking down corn stalks as they went. They ran down the gravel road toward the neighbors. Every which way they scattered, running off the pounds that they had gained to be marketable. Disaster was upon us.

Three hours later, after much labor, sweat, and yelling, we had the cattle back in their pen. Exhausted, the neighbors headed home, and I headed for the shower. As my father walked away with a tired face and voice, he said, "Son, daily check the fences and mend them if they need repair. It often only takes minutes to repair a fence. It takes hours to round up the cattle."

How often as I was growing up I had heard this sage advice from those wise with experience: "An ounce of prevention is worth a pound of cure." What we needed were some of the old-time radio and TV cowboys. They would have rounded up the cattle in no time at all. Roy Rogers, Gene Autry, Jimmy Stewart, and John Wayne just were not there when I needed them most.

The fence around the feedlot kept the cattle confined where they could gain the weight to potentially produce those delightful and delectable steaks, roasts, hamburgers, etc. The fence also kept predators from harming the cattle—predators like wild dogs and thieves.

I love the book of Nehemiah. It is one of my favorite Old Testament books. Nehemiah quickly recognized that without the walls of Jerusalem being rebuilt, all kinds of enemies could destroy the remnant of the Israelites. Fence mending became his top priority.

God wants us to keep the fences mended around our souls, hearts, and minds. When Jonah broke down the fence of God's will for his life, he spent three days eating raw fish and drinking gastric juices.

Proverbs 4:23 states, "Above all else, guard your heart, for it is the wellspring of life." God is saying "keep the fences around your heart mended. You must guard against the evil that can enter or the good than can depart from your heart when the fences are broken down."

Peter knew of the need to keep the fences around our lives strong and mended when he wrote, "Be well-balanced—temperate, sober-minded; be vigilant and cautious at all times, for that enemy of yours, the devil, roams around like a lion roaring [in fierce hunger], seeking someone to seize upon and devour" (I Peter 5:8, Amplified Bible).

Paul, writing to the Ephesians, states that for protection from the crafty, deceiving devil himself, we need total body protection. The armor Paul describes covers a believer from the top of his head to his toes. Plainly speaking, by putting on the whole armor of God, a believer has built a wall around himself, and the only way the devil can do any damage is if the wall breaks down and isn't mended.

I often think of how our spiritual lives are like the three parts that make a good fence. First, a basic part of the fence is the post that holds the fence upright and anchors it to the ground. Jesus is (or should be) the anchor in our lives. As the songwriter wrote, ". . . grounded firm and deep in the Savior's love."

Second, the fence itself is God's Word. Its commandments, promises, examples, etc. provide us with parameters and a safety zone for a life of prosperity, health, peace, and joy. "My son, do not forget my teaching, But let your heart keep my commandments; For length of days and years of life, And peace they will add to you. It will be healing to your body, And refreshment to your bones" (Proverbs 3:1-2,8, NAS). It also keeps out our enemies of fleshly desires, pride, idolatry, and sins of all nature. The Bible is replete with examples of those who went beyond the fences of God's truths and His will, and the terrible price they paid; e.g., the children of Israel in the book of Judges, Samson, Saul, David, Solomon, and the list goes on.

Third, a good fence is held in place by staples or fasteners. The fasteners in our lives should be prayer and meditation. The power of prayer is well known by those who fervently pray. The power of meditation is often overlooked. Joshua said that for true success and prosperity, one needed to spend time in meditation (Joshua 1:8). Prayer and meditation help us keep the right focus in our spiritual lives; a focus upon God's Word and will for our lives. God's Word, prayer, and meditation tell us where the fences need to be mended and how. In America today, the walls and fences that should protect us from within or without have crumbled or been torn down. Like a rampaging flood, all kinds of debauchery and sin have poured into the life of our nation and lives of families and individuals.

Parents whose lives should be a strong, spiritual "fence" around their children's lives are broken down. Their lives are ones of moral bankruptcy and ethical depravity. Marital infidelity and divorce can break down the fences around a child's life as quickly as snow melts on a sunny day.

The moral fences around our homes are broken down because of spiritual indifference, secular humanism, materialism, greed, dishonesty and certainly the immoral garbage that flows from the sewer of television. Scattered across the countryside is the carnage of broken homes and lives, all because we failed to keep the fences and walls mended.

How are the fences and walls around your soul, heart, and mind—your very being? How are the fences and walls around your home? Are they strong, or in need of repair?

EXAMPLE

"...EXAMPLE IS ALWAYS CLEAR."

Let no man despise thy youth; but be thou an example of the believers, in word, in conversation, in charity, in spirit, in faith, in purity.

I Timothy 4:12 (KJV)

"The eye is a more ready pupil than ever was the ear; good advice is often confusing; but example is always clear."

—Author Unknown

"Sir, if you will come into the back room, we have a few games in which you can participate. You could win a lot of money."

With those words, the sleazy-looking, crafty-eyed man invited my father into a room filled with gambling machines and card games. For a moment my Dad looked into the gambling den, and then he turned to the would-be thief and said, "No, thank you. I do not gamble. And more importantly, I will not set that type of

EXAMPLE   129

evil example for my wife and four children." With those words said, Dad turned away, and we all went back to the car and left.

The year was 1946. World War II had ended just a year before, and people were once again traveling. For several months, Dad and Mom had planned a trip to the Rocky Mountains and the Pacific Ocean.

On an August morning they filled our 1939 Dodge with suitcases, cooking utensils, sleeping bags and blankets, a cooking stove, soaps, food, and finally us four kids ranging in age from seven to thirteen (I was eleven). Dad put more into that car than most people get in their big SUV's today.

With a farewell wave to pets and neighbors, Dad eased our overloaded car onto the road, and we began an adventurous three-week trip. By noon, three hours after we left at the "reckless" speed of fifty miles per hour, we had arrived at the south side of Chicago (a trip that now takes only an hour and a half by interstate).

By mid-afternoon we had crossed Illinois, the mighty Mississippi River, and were traveling through Iowa, the land of corn, hogs, and cattle.

Then the signs appeared: "Just Ahead, Dangerous Reptiles." "See the Longest Snake in the World." "Stop and See the Most Unusual Reptiles." Mom and Dad were silent, hoping we didn't see the signs. But we did.

"Please stop!" we said in unison. "We want to see those big, bad reptiles," we begged.

As Dad slowed down, our excitement sped up in what seemed to be a direct correlation. We bounded out of the car as it stopped. Some of the reptiles were pretty ferocious looking, and the snake was probably the longest in the state of Iowa, but not the world. It was probably my first encounter with false advertising. But, it was a relief to be out of the crowded car.

Then, the shyster hit on Dad to gamble. For a moment I was afraid; I was afraid Dad would gamble all our trip money away, and we would be stranded in Iowa forever. But, he soon became my hero when he set a godly example, saying, "No, I will not set a bad example for my family."

This wasn't the only time Dad set a godly, moral example. Fast forward the clock six years. I was seventeen, already out of high school, and farming with Dad. Because we had a lot of livestock and were unable to grow enough feed, we sometimes bought corn from our neighboring farmers.

I had taken our farm truck to one of our neighbors and filled it with corn from his corn crib. Because most farmers had no scales, I drove to the nearest local grain elevator (four miles). After weighing the truck loaded with corn, I returned home to unload. After emptying the truck, I told Dad that the truck was low in gas and that I would fill the tank from our on-farm gasoline storage before I went back to the elevator to weigh the empty truck.

"Son, wait a minute; put only a few gallons in it. If you fill it up, the truck will weigh considerably more than when you first weighed."

"But, Dad," I protested, "at best it would only be equivalent to two bushels of corn." We paid $1.25 per bushel. Dad's sober look ended the conversation. I did as I was told. He set a good and godly example over $2.50 worth of corn.

EXAMPLE   131

I have never forgotten these two moral examples set by an honest Dad. "There is transcendent power in example. We reform others unconsciously, when we walk upright" (Author unknown). Dad was a farmer, not a preacher. He knew one can preach a better sermon with his life than with his lips.

The Bible uses the word "example" only nine times, but every major character (and many minor characters) set examples by their lives and actions. Adam and Eve set an example of disobedience; Noah of godly perseverance; Moses of long-suffering leadership; Abraham of obedience; Joseph of moral courage; Joshua of courage; David of both a good love of God and a bad lust of flesh; Solomon of both good wisdom and bad foolishness; Daniel of youthful moral character; Jesus as a suffering Savior; and Peter, John, and Paul of persevering, suffering evangelists.

The list could go on for many pages. Many of their words are great: the Psalms of David, the Proverbs of Solomon, and the teachings of Jesus, but it is their lives that make them our examples—our heroes.

Sadly, in today's culture there are far more bad, immoral examples than good ones. Parents set the wrong examples of cursing and mocking spiritual things; of alcoholism; of selfishness and greed; and of anger, vindictiveness, and bitterness. Government leaders set examples of immorality, greed, corruption, falsehood, and lies.

Today's heroes for millions of both young and old alike are movie or TV performers, so-called music entertainers, and athletes whose lives are morally bankrupt, filled with immorality, drug addiction, and worse of all, a hatred for God, family, country and righteousness, truth, and justice. Like an infectious disease, immoral examples are making our society desperately sick.

The philosopher Balguy wrote, "Whatever parent gives his children good instruction, and sets them at the same time a bad example, may be considered as bringing them food in one hand, and poison in the other."

It is not wealth or education that will lift society out of its current immoral, corrupt state. It will be the godly example of great and pure individuals who will lift us to noble, biblical thoughts and deeds.

Thanks, Dad and Mom. Of all the gifts you gave me, the best was a godly example.

Parents, what kind of example are you setting for your children?

FRONT PORCH

"No Need for a Psychiatrist"

And by the hands of the apostles were many signs and wonders wrought among the people; (and they were all with one accord in Solomon's porch).

Acts 5:12 (KJV)

A front porch on a house is one of God's great architectural creations. It serves many purposes: it protects a house from the cold, brutal winds of winter; it protects a house from the blazing heat of summer; it can keep you dry when it rains; it is a place where a person can read, write, meditate, pray, and even take a nap; it is a place where pets can be petted; and it is a place where snacks can be eaten and games played; where parents could rest after a hard day's work. Porches can be beautiful in architectural design. Flowers, and especially Boston ferns, can hang from the ceiling (I am not sure why Boston folks got the right to have both beans and ferns named after them). Containers filled with beautiful blooms can be placed at any location.

But, best of all, it provides a great place for fellowship: a place where family, friends, and neighbors can share God's blessings and resolve daily problems or even the world's problems; a place where lifetime friendships can be born; and a place where a person can put his (or her) thinking together.

Our family house had a porch that wrapped half-way around it. I spent many happy hours on it, doing many of the things I listed above. I noticed that those who fellowshipped on the front porch seldom had need for a psychiatrist. On the porch, problems were shared, discussed, and resolved, whether it be family members, neighbors, or friends. There God's blessings were shared, and all rejoiced. At times the porch was a place of conflict resolution, without an attorney.

I have noticed few poets have written poems about front porches. Even fewer philosophers have philosophized about front porches. Perhaps they never experienced the blessings and joy of a front porch. As a country boy experienced in "front porches," I can tell those poets and philosophers their writing would have been much greater if they had spent time in a rocking chair on a front porch.

As great as front porches are, they lead to something even greater—the house itself. I ate many snacks on the porch: home-made cookies, pieces of pie, glasses of milk, etc. But the real meals—breakfast, dinner, and supper—were served in the house. I took naps on an old Buffalo robe on the porch, but my comfortable bed was in the house. I loved to read on the porch, but the serious study took place in the house.

I have noticed that many Christians, or even would-be Christians, exercise this "porch vs. house"relationship. They read a few verses of Scripture (porch), but never seriously study and meditate upon God's Word (house). They attend church about half the time (porch), but never enter into a full fellowship of worship, study, church programs, and activities (house). They occasionally spend time with family, neighbors, and friends (porch), but seldom get deeply involved in leading their family and helping their neighbors (house). They give a few dollars in offerings (porch) and never fully tithe (house).

Revelation 3:14-19 is the godly rebuke to the Laodicean church. To a country boy philosopher, it appears those Laodiceans never left the front porch to go into the house. Scriptures, especially in the Gospels, record how many people came up on the porch in following Jesus, but then they turned and left, never entering into full fellowship with Jesus (house).

There is a porch/house parallel in dating and marriage. Young men and women spend many hours, days, months, even years, dating (porch), and then they get married (house).

As a consultant to Christian ministries, I taught leaders and development personnel developmental "porch activities." These were activities that introduced parents, grandparents, and the community in general to a ministry that would lead them eventually to coming into the "house" with the full support of children, prayer, time, and finances.

My memories of the front porch are still refreshing, even today. The many activities that took place there have enriched my life. Parents, if you don't have a front porch on your house, build one. Put a couple of rocking chairs on it and wave good-bye to the psychiatrists.

STEWARDSHIP OF TIME

"Please, Turn Off Television"

I will set no worthless thing before my eyes;
I hate the work of those who fall away;
it shall not fasten its grip on me.

Psalm 101:3 (NAS)

"What was the thing for which you were most thankful as you grew up?"

The question was posed to me by a budding journalism class. I was administrator of a Christian school, and part of the journalism students' assignments was to be a reporter and interview people. Seated in my office, with paper and pen ready, they anxiously awaited my reply. Was a newfound truth or new revelation forthcoming?

"My Christian parents are for what I am most thankful," I replied. Then pausing, I reflected, "And the fact we had no television in our home."

The students' pens momentarily halted. They looked up, and their expressions seemed to say, "How did you ever survive without TV?"

"I love to read, have a curious mind, and am a creative person today because we had no television in our home as I grew up," I responded.

With disbelief, they wrote my response, not sure they should report something so weird. The students must have been thinking, "How could he have been educated and hold an administrator's position, having been deprived of television in his childhood years?" Would the readers of their writing think it was fiction rather than fact?

I saw my first television show(s) in my junior year in high school (1951).

"Mom, can I stay in town and watch television at Uncle Ellis and Aunt Edna's plumbing store?" I asked. They had a small black and white TV set in their store, and after they closed on Saturday night (about 9:00 p.m.), they would watch pro wrestling. "Please, Mom, they said they would bring me home," I pleaded.

With Mom's approval, I ran to their store and spent an hour watching the partially put-on show of professional wrestling. Even back then, as today, it was part show to draw and entertain an audience, and part (small part) real wrestling. Why my uncle and aunt had a television set in their store and not in their home, I will never know. They seemed to be just ordinary folks with no skeletons in their closets. The way I look at it, it's just one of those "mysteries of life."

At the time I was growing up, I didn't recognize that having no television was a heaven-sent blessing. Upon reflection, I now know that my love for reading and my reading skills, my curious mind of always wanting to learn, my creative skills, my people-oriented personality, my work ethic, and my physical strength are due largely to having had no television in our home.

As I remember back to a time when a nation, a community, a family, a person was TV-free, I am overwhelmed by the many negative influences it has brought.

There have been many studies and much research done in the past twenty years about the detrimental effect of TV upon our lives, and especially upon children. Here are a few of the research results:

*   In one year, children (students) watch 1,500 hours of television, compared to approximately 900 hours in school

*   The average American watches four hours of TV each day

*   There is an average of three TV's in an American home

*   Almost 70% of Americans have the TV set on while eating dinner (supper)

*   Parents spend less than forty minutes per week in any kind of meaningful conversation with their children

*   Over 50% of children ages 5-17 have a TV in their bedroom

*   Over 25% of children ages 2-5 have a TV in their bedroom

*   By the time a child finishes elementary school, they have seen over 8,000 murders

*   By age 18, children have seen over 200,000 acts of violence and 16,000 murders

Beyond any shadow of a doubt, TV research has shown that children think problems can be solved through violence. TV has been an evil force to destroy moral character, mental capabilities, reading ability, creative logical thinking, a good work ethic, and physical health/strength.

In a recent survey, one-third of all prison inmates said TV had a definite influence on their doing evil deeds. TV addiction is a reality for millions of both children and adults.

No one seems to have an answer as to why parents allow something that spews forth vulgarity and profanity, anti-God, anti-country, anti-family, and immoral values in their home. If someone came to their door spewing forth cursing and debauchery, they would not be invited in. Perhaps that is why TV has been called "the uninvited guest."

In the early 1980s, an organization was started called TV Turnoff Network. It challenged families and schools to turn off TV for one week. The students and parents signed a contract that they would turn off TV for a week. Those who did were greatly rewarded. The feedback was amazing. Reading revivals broke out, family communications noticeably increased, family games and activities sprang forth, student grades improved, and students reported getting A's on exams, which had never happened to them before (a little study always helps). Family life returned to normal—even exceptional, as one parent stated. The most meaningful activities in the family are often those simple interactions that build lasting connections between generations, the type of activities and interactions that seldom take place when a family is continually "glued" to the TV.

Many families went on beyond the week and stayed totally TV-free. One family I know took their TV into the backyard, and with the family standing back, Dad took a shotgun and blew the TV's "guts" out. They then buried the TV and prayed over the grave. As the Dad said, "It was a prayer of thanksgiving that God had delivered them from the evil influence TV had been upon their lives." I told him I thought his actions were perhaps a bit extreme and dramatic, to which he said, "My children will not forget how we rid our family of the tentacles of TV." I could only say "Amen."

Lest you, the reader, think by now I am totally against TV, I am not. I believe God allowed man to create TV for a good purpose. There are certainly some good programs on TV, programs that are informative, educational, of human interest, entertaining, etc. TV "church" can minister to the elderly, invalid, sick, those who are confined to their homes and can't go to their local church services. Then there are many classic movies like "It's a Wonderful Life" and "Gone With the Wind" that provide wholesome entertainment.

As a boy growing up, I often wondered about the two witnesses for God spoken of in Revelation chapter 11. In verse 9 it indicates the whole world will see their witnessing, death, and resurrection. Since the invention of TV and its world-wide reach, I understand how this could happen. Paul, writing to the Ephesians, states ". . . making the most of your time, because the days are evil" (Ephesians 6:16, NAS).

God wants us to be good stewards of our treasures (money), our talents, and our time. No doubt, TV has become a big time waster for millions of children and adults. It has definitely desensitized us to sin and immoral values. Time is one of God's gifts to us. It can't be saved or bought; it can only be spent. God wants us to spend our time wisely.

I must confess that I spend too much time watching TV. Most of my watching is the Weather Channel (my daughter-in-law says I am addicted to this channel), History Channel, or sporting events; and to my shame, I spend more time watching TV than studying God's Word, reading spiritually-oriented books, and participating in spiritually-oriented activities. As a friend of mine said, "If you want to turn your mind to mush, let your muscles grow flabby, and balloon your weight, spend a lot of time watching TV."

Parents, do you want to take back your time and family? Then turn off the TV.

WOODEN TOYS

"Whether a Man or a Boy, He Is Known by the Size of His Toys."

When I was a child, I talked like a child, I thought like a child, I reasoned like a child; now that I have become a man, I am done with childish ways and have put them aside.

I Corinthians 13:11 (Amplified)

It was 5:00 a.m. on a Christmas morning. I had awakened with eager anticipation. Did Santa (Dad) bring me an electric train? Slowly I crept down the steps and peeked around the corner into the living room. There it was! Under the Christmas tree was the electric train I so desired: an engine, four freight cars, and a caboose on an oval track, and even a short tunnel. A dream come true!

Dad and Mom were still sleeping (I think Dad was tired from playing with the train after he set it up). As quiet as I could, I started playing with the train. As it circled the track, I knew I was in "train heaven." I could imagine myself as an engineer on a real steam train. I was holding the throttle and racing down the track at sixty miles per hour, blowing the whistle. I had to bring the train in on time. As I flew past the crossings, both children and adults waved to me. The toy train catapulted me into an imaginary life as an engineer: the one who could bring the train in on time to its destination. At only seven years old, I already had a creative mind that took me from a boy playing with his new Christmas toy to an imaginary world.

Soon, Mom and Dad were awake. They and my three siblings joined me around the Christmas tree. After the Bible story of the birth of Christ was read and gifts exchanged, Mom departed to the kitchen to fix a hearty Christmas breakfast.

"Mom, can you bring my breakfast into the living room?" I asked. "I don't want to leave the train."

Needless to say, the request was emphatically denied. It was either play with the train or eat.

"But Mom, sometimes real train engineers skip meals to bring the train in on time," I argued. One look at Dad's face told me I should depart immediately for the kitchen.

During the winter months that followed, the train provided many hours of great pleasure. Then, spring came.

"Mom, can I take the train set out into the yard?"

"No, Son, the yard is too soft to support it properly; and besides, we do not have an electric cord long enough to supply the power."

Then my creative mind went to work. To the woodpile I went. I selected chunks of wood that would make a train—a piece that looked like an engine, some pieces that looked like freight cars, and one that could be a caboose.

"Dad, I need a hammer, some nails, string, small pieces of wood, and a saw."

With a quizzical look he asked, "Why?"

"I am building a wooden train," I emphatically responded.

Wanting to laugh and yet not destroy my boyish creativity, he granted my request. Soon I had the wooden train built and was pulling it across the yard. One of my brothers laughed, along with Dad and Mom. They said it didn't look like a train; obviously they didn't have the superior creative mind I had.

My grandfather operated a sawmill for many years. He had twenty or more different customers who bought his lumber. Three of them were wooden toy manufacturers. During the last quarter of the nineteenth century and the first half of the twentieth century (1875-1950), most toys were wooden, thus providing my grandfather and others with a ready market for their lumber. Wooden toys were durable and had a long life. Usually a child would get only one toy for Christmas. So, it had to last for at least a year.

A year earlier, I had received a wooden tractor and wagon. The year following the gift of the electric train, I received a wooden TinkerToy set and the next year, a Lincoln Logs set. They lasted several years and provided many hours of creative building.

It was 1941 when I received the train set. Money and goods were scarce. The severe depression of the 1930s still lingered, and only a few weeks earlier, World War II had started for the United States. As I reflect back to that Christmas, I know Dad and Mom made some real sacrifices so we children could have at least one toy each.

How different it was then compared to our supposedly modern culture. When one walks through the toy section aisles in Wal-Mart, K-Mart or Toys-R-Us, the choices and prices are overwhelming: toys that cost up to many hundreds of dollars; toys that cost as much as what one used to pay for "forty acres and a mule."

Recently I attended a birthday party. The birthday girl received over twenty gifts ranging in value from a few dollars to over two hundred dollars. After the birthday celebrant had opened all her gifts, she started playing with an empty box in which a gift had come. She pretended it was a play house. After we left the party, my wife and I decided that from now on, we would give only empty boxes for birthday and Christmas gifts. I have been in homes where a child has received gift after gift for Christmas or birthday, and an hour later are whining they have nothing to do.

What Paul writes in the eleventh verse of I Corinthians 13 intrigues me. The previous ten verses focus on the supremacy of love. Is Paul saying focus on what is, or should be, top priority in our lives? I think so. Paul is saying that our #1 priority should be to love God with all our hearts; to love His Word; to love our spouse, to love our children, to love our church, and certainly to love our neighbors. This shows spiritual maturity whether as a church collectively or as an individual. Then in verse 11 I believe he is saying

STOP spending your talent, time, and money on childish things that have no eternal value—the things of the world that capture our life, our soul, our heart, our mind, our emotions, and certainly our money. Paul tells us to GROW UP, stop being childish and spending our time, talents, and money on low-cost or no-value things.

On the day of an Amish wedding, there is a ceremony that usually lasts all morning. At noon there is a large feast as only the Dutch and German women can provide, a meal almost beyond description, with its long tables of all kinds of home-cooked food and delicacies. The children and young people, along with the new bride and groom, join in an afternoon of the fun games and other activities. Once the wedding day is over, the newly-married couple should no longer participate in youthful games and activities. They are to now "grow up" and begin building a home and family.

Jesus said, "For where your treasure is, there will your heart be also" (Matthew 6:21, KJV). It has been often said, "A record of a person's expenditures will tell where his heart is." While Christian ministries and individual families lack needed funding, I have seen men spend huge sums of money on "big boy toys" (e.g., cars, trucks, boats, hobbies, collections). What a spiritually immature and bankrupt culture we live in when billions of dollars are spent each year on childish things, leaving ministries and families financially anemic.

Even today I cherish the memory of the toy train on that Christmas day. Since then I have had the pleasure of riding in the cab of a steam engine many times. It was fun, but not as glamorous as I dreamed as a seven-year-old boy. A steam engine cab is hot in the summer and cold in the winter—and always dirty. Nevertheless, I still enjoy being around the train environment today. Railroading is my main hobby. At times it has gone beyond where it belongs, and God has had to remind me to put away "childish" things and focus on His will of love and obedience for me.

How our culture, our thinking, our priorities, our actions have changed; from a child receiving one toy for Christmas and having it bring hours of happiness, to a child receiving a myriad of toys yet feeling bored and unhappy. From a man dedicated to providing for his family, neighbor's, and church's needs, to one who spends thousands of dollars for "big boy toys."

Thanks, Mom and Dad, for just one toy that brought lasting memories I still cherish today. Moms and Dads, are your priorities "childish" or "grown up?" Are you helping your children become spiritually mature or harmfully spoiled?

DIRT POOR

"Poor Materially — Rich Spiritually"

But godliness actually is a means of great gain, when accompanied by contentment.

I Timothy 6:6 (NAS)

"Son, get back into this house and get your shoes on. It is winter time! You will catch a cold or even worse, the flu."

"But, Mom," I quickly retorted, "John and Henry go outside without shoes even in the winter time."

"That's because they are DIRT POOR. Now get back in here," Mom said.

"Wait a minute, Mom. Our soil is rich, productive, and deep. It is not 'poor.' What do you mean by dirt poor?"

With a sigh, Mom motioned for me to come back into the house. After I was seated in a warm kitchen with some hot chocolate and a freshly-baked cookie, she explained, "Dirt poor is an expression used to describe people who have very little money, live in small, rundown houses, raise much of the food they eat, and have little in the way of clothing, especially new."

I was puzzled. "But, Mom, if they are 'dirt poor' as you say, then why are they two of the happiest families in our church?"

Mom, with a look of spiritual wisdom, softly answered, "Son, they are poor in earthly things, but very rich in heavenly things."

Now I was even more puzzled. Mom, seeing that questioning look on my face, got her Bible and turned to I Timothy, Chapter 6 (KJV). Slowly she read, "But godliness with contentment is great gain." She looked up. "You see, son, they have very little by the world's standards, yet they are very thankful for and content with what God has given them."

On that cold, dreary day, when I had attempted to go outside barefooted, I had gained a new insight about my two friends, John and Henry. They were both a part of large families. Both families lived in similar circumstances. John's family of six (two parents and four children) lived in a small, run-down house. It had a very small kitchen, a dining room, three small bedrooms (one for the parents, one for two boys, and one for two girls), and a covered back porch that was full of clutter and seemed about to fall down. The house exterior had old, weathered boards that barely kept out the cold winter winds. There was a small, run-down barn that housed their old and rusty Studebaker car, a sad-looking milk cow, a few pigs, and several chickens. Around the house, there were very few shrubs (that always seemed to be dying), and the small lawn was mostly crab grass and weeds. The best-looking thing about the whole place was their garden. It was big and full of all kinds of spring, summer, and fall vegetables. When it came to food, they ate like kings. Why, they even bordered their garden with beautiful flowers. Their garden sure did "dress up" an otherwise drab, dreary place.

On Sunday nights in our small, country church, there was always time for testimonies. John's parents were among the first to give praise for how good God was to them. Even the kids, on an occasion, shared how God was blessing their lives. John seemed to be one of the happiest kids in school, even though he wore hand-me-down clothes from an older brother.

Henry's family was also large. Really large. There were twelve, with two parents and ten children. It seemed they were even poorer than John's family. Their house was an old log cabin with the cracks filled in with mortar and strips of plywood. The lane to their house was a quarter mile in length and was full of holes seemingly always filled with water, mud, and ice. The kids walked the lane every school day to meet the bus and return home again in the evening. The weather-beaten barn and few other out buildings were badly in need of paint and repair. They also kept a milk cow, some pigs, and chickens, which gave them a constant supply of fresh milk and eggs along with fresh meat. Their car was worn, rusty, noisy, and run-down but always seemed to work when needed. They also had a huge garden that supplied much of their food needs.

The mother and the kids spent much of the summer and fall growing and canning the abundance of the garden. One time when I visited Henry, his dad showed me a rather large wagon filled (twenty bushels or more) with soup beans he had raised. He said that was a part of their winter food supply. He claimed there was nothing better than a meal of soup beans, with some ham and onions mixed in it, and homemade cornbread, all of which were home grown. I agreed. For many years, I have enjoyed this simple, God-given meal. Today it is a specialty item on Cracker Barrel's menu.

Henry's dad was always in demand by local merchants and farmers to help them, because he was honest and very conscientious in his work ethic. But, Henry's dad could neither read nor write. His wife and their kids read to him often, usually from the Bible, and by candlelight or kerosene lamps. The family did not have electricity or running water in the house. Yet, in spite of their earthly circumstances, Henry's dad was always first on his feet at our country church to sing; yes, actually sing his testimony of God's greatness and goodness in his booming, bass voice that would rattle the windows of the church.

As the years have gone by, I have rubbed elbows with many wealthy people and families, and have been in their homes: huge houses with all the latest in electronic conveniences and amusements, where every child has his or her own large bedroom filled with all the latest electronic devices; and where there are large swimming pools, elaborate, opulent landscaping (including ponds and waterfalls), and acres of lawn and flowers. Often I have found among these people strife, greed, bitterness, deceit, deception, broken families, disobedient children, drug users, alcoholics—in short, little happiness and much sorrow. Never have I found families with godly contentment as I found in the two "dirt poor" families with whom I grew up.

Today's humanistic, godless culture and societal philosophies have produced greed, selfishness, bitterness, envy, and covetousness that knows no bounds. The almighty dollar is god and king. We have a society where people spend far beyond their means for things that do not satisfy the mind, heart, and soul.

On that cold November morning, as I attempted to go barefooted on frozen ground, Mom began the process of my learning the true meaning of I Timothy 6:6-8 (KJV): "But godliness with contentment is great gain; For we brought nothing into this world, and it is certain we can carry nothing out. And having food and raiment let us be therewith content."

As the country wisdom-filled philosopher correctly stated, "There are no U-Haul trailers or trucks following the hearse."

Would you be content if you were "dirt poor"?

GOD KEEPS RECORD

"My Dad (and Other Farmers) Had the First 'Palm Pilots'"

Then I saw a great white throne and the One who was seated upon it, from whose presence and from the sign of whose face earth and sky fled away and no place was found for them. I [also] saw the dead, great and small; they stood before the throne, and books were opened. Then another book was opened, which is [the Book] of Life. And the dead were judged (sentenced) by what they had done [their whole way of feeling and acting, their aims and endeavors] in accordance with what was recorded in the books.

Revelation 20:11-12 (Amplified)

Recently I watched several people, including my youngest son, using PDAs (Personal Data Assistants). You could tell from their bodily and facial expressions that they believed they were on the "cutting edge" of the most advanced technology. I could tell this by the way they held their Palm Pilots(TM) deliberately, for everyone to see, and the serious, studious, proud look on their faces.

Well, I have news for these high-tech "yuppies"—my dad and other farmers had "Palm Pilots" as far back as one hundred years ago. I shall explain.

To fully understand the early "Palm Pilots," one must first understand the role of bib overalls. The bib overall was one of God's great creations for farmers (and their wives), and railroad engineers. The bib overall had deep rear pockets for big red handkerchiefs; big front pockets to carry pocket knives, twine, nails, bolts and many other useful things; a loop on the side of one leg to carry a hammer; and a pocket on the side of the other leg to carry a wooden folding ruler or whatever.

However, the most important pockets were at the top, the bib part of the overalls at chest height. There were two pockets, side by side, in which the farmers carried their "personal data assistants." You see, it was there they carried their little spiral-bound notebooks. These notebooks were usually given to the farmers by a seed, feed, fertilizer, or farm machinery company for advertising purposes. Between the pockets was a pencil-sized pocket where a pencil was carried, again usually from a feed, seed, fertilizer, or farm machinery business. So, when a farmer wanted to record anything, all he had to do was reach into one of his pockets and get his "Palm Pilot" notebook. There he would record such things as:

1. What date he put the bull with the cows or the boar with the sows (for mating purposes) to give him an idea when the "little ones" would be born

2. What variety of corn, oats, or so forth that he planted in a field and the date

3. What he needed in supplies the next time he went to town

4. What the agreement was when he purchased some grain, a cow, pig or horse from a neighbor

5. What the grain yields were from his last harvest; i.e., bushels per acre

6. The date when he last kissed his wife

7. And much more.

These early "palm pilot" notebooks were so advanced that they contained a wealth of information; e.g., advance yearly calendars, weights and measures of all major grains and liquids, important dates and holidays, and when the next full moon would be (moon phases sometimes dictated the best planting times).

Why, with two palm-pilot-pockets in those bib overalls, it was not uncommon for many farmers to have two "Palm Pilot" notebooks; it was a "badge of honor" to have two.

Although it was my Dad who carried the notebook, it was my Mom who occasionally and gently reminded me that God was also a record keeper. Between observing Dad write relevant information in his notebook and Mom's reminders of Scripture, I began to understand that my actions, deeds, and even my thoughts were being recorded by God.

There are numerous examples of Scripture where God has recorded (taken note of) certain actions by mankind that brought about judgment. In Genesis 6, verses 5-7, the sinful actions of man were seen and recorded by God, resulting in the Great Flood. God saw and recorded the sinful actions of the children of Israel, and Moses, in their journey from Egypt to the Promised Land, and Joshua and Caleb were the only members of the adult generation to enter the "new home." The rest perished in the wastelands of the desert. Moses, in his farewell speech to the Israelites, asks God to record the fact that he set before them a choice of life or death; blessing or cursing (Deut. 30:19 and 31:28).

Perhaps the greatest example of how God keeps record is found in I Samuel 15:2 (KJV): "Thus saith the LORD of hosts, I remember that which Amalek did to Israel, how he laid wait for him in the way, when he came up from Egypt." Approximately 400 years after the Amalekites had harassed and hindered the Israelites as they journeyed to the Promised Land, God remembered. He literally recorded what had happened. God finally brought their record to bear against them with eventual utter destruction.

Six times in the book of John, He says "I bear record, I have recorded for you the truth and reality of the working of the Holy Spirit; the truth of Jesus being the Son of God; the despair and desperation of the Crucifixion; and the glorious triumph of the Resurrection."

In Revelation 1:12 (KJV), John states, "The Revelation of Jesus Christ, which God gave unto him, to show unto his servants things which must shortly come to pass; and he sent and signified it by his angel unto his servant, John, Who bore witness of the word of God, and of the testimony of Jesus Christ, and of all things that he saw." John clearly states that all that follows in this book is a record that God keeps in heaven about His Son, Jesus Christ and the future of mankind, now revealed to him.

The Bible itself is God's record of His perfect creation; man's fall into sin; His plan of redemption through Jesus Christ; the birth of His church and the future of mankind; the earth; and even the starry heavens. God has revealed to us all these things through His written record, His Holy Word.

So, all you young "high-tech yuppies," you are not as much on the cutting edge as you think. As a matter of fact, those early "palm pilots" never needed battery replacements and never crashed, as yours frequently do.

God's method of record keeping is omniscient and far superior to the palm pilot or pocket notebook. The question must be asked, "What has He recorded about you?"

WELL FED

"THREE SQUARE MEALS A DAY"

And ye shall eat in plenty, and be satisfied, and praise the name of the LORD your God, that hath dealt wondrously with you; and my people shall never be ashamed.

Joel 2:26 (KJV)

M om always attempted to feed us three square meals every day. Not only did she insist upon regular times for meals (breakfast at 7:00 a.m., dinner at noon, and supper at 6:00 p.m.), but she also insisted upon and prepared balanced meals. There was home-grown meat for protein and plenty of fresh, garden-raised vegetables for the energy-giving carbohydrates, vitamins, minerals, etc. There was home-made bread on which to spread the home-churned butter and jams or jellies, to furnish us with sufficient amounts of vitamin A, large glasses of milk for calcium and vitamin D, and then came those home-made desserts: cakes, pies, and cookies for our "sweet tooth."

Mom was a master and sometimes even a genius at making sure we had three square meals a day. Occasionally, Dad or one of us kids would do or plan something that would interfere with her schedule. We soon experienced her wrath, and we refrained from interfering with her strong motherly desire to give us three square and balanced meals a day.

During the spring months, Mom worked many hours preparing and planting a large garden. During the summer and fall months, she spent hundreds of hours canning the bountiful produce of the garden (we had no freezer at that time), and then during the winter months, she could still put three square meals a day on the table. Mom knew that we needed a lot of energy and strength to help Dad with all the farm chores. We were his "hired hands." Mom and Dad, by preparing and storing food for the winter, were living examples of the biblical illustration of the ant as found in Proverbs 6:6-8.

On occasion, Mom would say, "Like I want you to have three square meals a day, even more God wants you to have three square meals a day." As a child, that statement puzzled me.

"How can God feed us like Mom?" I questioned.

As I have grown in wisdom over the years, I now understand the biblical principle Mom was teaching by her example. God wants us to have three square meals a day by constantly and consistently feeding on His Word. The psalmist proclaimed, "O taste and see that the Lord is good..." (Psalm 34:8, KJV). God wants to feed us on a regular basis. As I had regular meals at the family table, so God wants us to be regularly in His Word, feasting upon its riches in a daily manner.

Jesus, in His simple, yet profound prayer, said, "Give us this day our daily bread" (Matthew 6:11, KJV).

In the book of Acts we read that the early church grew rapidly because converts were daily learning and proclaiming the Word (Acts 2:46–47). Daily, regular devotions have been proven to be a great way to be fed by the Word.

God's Word and meditation upon it is spiritual meat, potatoes, bread, vegetables, fruit pies, cakes, and cookies to feed our souls. The psalmist urges us to feed on God's Word, "How sweet are thy words unto my taste! Yea sweeter than honey to my mouth" (Psalm 119:103, KJV).

As Mom's three square meals a day made us physically healthy and strong, so feeding upon God's Word makes us spiritually healthy and strong.

By today's culinary standards and practices, our tastes and habits have been perverted by the fast food industry. We want hamburgers and fries, when it should be veggies and fruits. Sadly, I don't think a "McVeggies" will do well financially. We need to get back to the joyful ecstasies of real food as God and Mom made it, back to three square meals a day.

Many people eat more junk food between meals than wholesome foods at regular meals. Much research by scientists and nutritional experts has proven that regular meals, eaten slowly and consisting of nutritious foods, promotes good health. Mom knew the benefits of "three square meals a day" many years before research proved it. She sure did have a lot of God-given wisdom about feeding her family!

As we digested those three square meals a day, we received the needed strength to perform our duties. We should not only feed upon God's Word, but we should meditate upon it, for out of meditation comes the understanding, strength and motivation to do God's will and work. "This book of the law shall not depart out of thy mouth; but thou shalt meditate therein day and night, that thou mayest observe to do according to all that is written therein; for then thou shalt make thy way prosperous, and then thou shalt have good success" (Joshua 1:8, KJV); "But his delight is in the law of the LORD; and in his law doth he meditate day and night" (Psalm 1:2, KJV).

It is interesting that both of these books begin by commanding us not to just read God's Word, but to meditate upon it. It is the meditation upon God's Word that gives us the strength for God's "chores." In today's culture, we eat fast food at a fast pace; we have fast devotions followed by fast meditation. Our churches provide us with fast teaching and preaching. Our appetites are satisfied, but our souls go hungry.

Do you have three square meals a day both spiritually and physically?

HARD WORK

"The Sweet Smell of Sweat"

*By the sweat of your brow you will eat your food until you
return to the ground, since from it you were taken; for dust
you are and to dust you will return.*

Genesis 3:19

"Jim, come here. I want to give you a hug."

Oh, no, I think. I don't want a hug from my hug-loving
aunt.

She raises her arms to hug me, draws me close, and then I smell
it. The smell of sweat coming from her armpits. YUK! But, it's
too late; I can't get out of it. I must suffer through another hug
under the arms of my aunt.

Southerners are more "huggy" than Northerners (Yankees). I
am not sure why my aunt was so "huggy." I know she was not
Southern, but somewhere she had adopted the Southern culture of
hugging.

It was bad enough for an eight-year-old boy who believed hugs
were only for sissies; but to be hugged by someone who smelled of
sweat—that was the ultimate embarrassment for a boy who wanted

to portray an image of being "mean" and "tough." If I could have, I would have worn a sign that said "No Hugs Allowed."

I grew up in a time before Old Spice deodorant was created and before the deodorant companies produced and sold millions of products, generating a billion-dollar industry. It was a time when, "if you raised your arms, you truly did lose your charms." A good bath or just a wash rag could remove the sweat smell temporarily, but soon it would return, especially during periods of hot weather.

As I grew older, I began to understand that the smell of sweat was associated with hard work—work by honest, God-fearing men and women. They understood the importance of a good work ethic. When employed by others, they gave eight hours of hard work for eight hours of pay. From the book of Proverbs, they had learned that poverty comes to those who are lazy. The Bible does not use our modern-day word "lazy," but rather the word slothful, of which there are seventeen references, forty percent alone being in the book of Proverbs. "I went by the field of the slothful, and by the vineyard of the man void of understanding; And lo, it was all grown over with thorns, and nettles had covered the face thereof, and the stone wall thereof was broken down. Then I saw, and considered it well; I looked upon it, and received instruction. Yet a little sleep, a little slumber, a little folding of the hands to sleep; So shall thy poverty come as one that travelleth; and thy want as an armed man" (Proverbs 24:30-34, KJV). Also, the word sluggard is used six times, meaning a lazy person.

Medical doctors, health therapists, and other health-related personnel tell us that it is good to sweat. Sweating cools our bodies when we put forth great amounts of energy, whether in work, exercise, or play. The best-feeling shower in the world is a shower taken after a period of sweating.

My grandparents taught my parents a good work ethic. My parents taught me the same good work ethic. I, in turn, taught my children a good work ethic. This is the way it should be taught, from one generation to another. The teaching should come from both example and verbal instruction, with example being the best.

I lived in a community where I was surrounded by hard-working farmers and businessmen who set the example for me. My parents created and assigned work for me to do. There was carrying in the wood to fuel the furnace and stove. There were daily chores of caring for the livestock. There was the planting and harvesting of vegetables in and from the garden. There was the picking of the fruit from the orchards. There was mending and building of fences. There was painting of the farm buildings. The list goes on.

In today's culture children, young people and many adults seem to have little or no work ethic. Parents, instead of teaching their children a good work ethic, have allowed them to learn the "garbage ethic." Their children are allowed to sit in front of a TV or computer, continually playing video games hour after hour, which too often fills their minds and hearts with garbage and fails to build a good work ethic.

The lack of a good work ethic among school students at all levels causes failing grades and dropouts. The curriculum is "dumbed-down" to meet the level of work ethic-deprived students. The work place; i.e., businesses, suffer because so many employees have a poor work ethic. They come from high schools and colleges and are employed, expecting eight hours of pay for two hours of work.

Those with poor work ethics spend their time on their latest cell phone texting, taking long breaks, and hiding in out-of-the-way places rather than working. Shame on parents who have failed to teach their children a good work ethic.

Adam and Eve, before they sinned, worked (without sweat) in the Garden of Eden. They named and cared for the animals, harvested their food, and possibly even cultivated and planted new and various vegetation.

"Success is ninety percent perspiration and ten percent inspiration." How true is that statement! I have noticed that success comes to those who have rolled up their sleeves and applied a good work ethic. Depression counselors urge those who are depressed to find a job or ministry, and work. Depression is depressed when one is busy with an activity or work. The great inventor Thomas Edison wrote, "As a cure for worrying, work is better than whiskey."

There are hundreds of references to work in Scripture; most of them have a positive connotation. God worked six days to create the marvelous world around us. Noah worked to build an ark of safety. Moses worked in leading the Israelites out of Egypt. Joshua worked to conquer Israel's enemies. Much work went into the building of the Tabernacle and Temple. Jesus worked daily, teaching and healing. Peter worked when he preached. Paul worked feverishly to plant churches. All the Old and New Testament writers worked. Scriptures are replete with instructions on how Christians should work—honestly, courageously, "as unto the Lord." Paul, writing to the Ephesians (4:28), told the thieves to stop stealing and go to work.

Humorists have joked about work. Jerome K. Jerome jokingly said, "I like work; it fascinates me. I can sit and look at it for hours." Work can be productive, worthwhile, boring, frustrating, harmful, fun, rewarding, necessary, heavy, light, physical, mental, emotional, and so forth. The philosopher Henry Giles summed it up best when he wrote, "Man must work. This is as certain as the sun. But he may work grudgingly, or he may work gratefully; He may work as a man, or he may work as a machine. There is no work so rude, that he may not exalt it; no work so impassive that he may not breathe a soul into it; no work so dull that he may not enliven it."

God ordained work and the sweat that comes with it, whether it be physical or mental. Parents, have you taught your children and grandchildren what the Bible says about work and a good work ethic? If you haven't, then I challenge you to start today.

Thanks, Dad and Mom, for teaching me a good work ethic.

A FIELD FULL OF WEEDS

"HELP! I AM BEING CHOKED TO DEATH!"

Other seed fell among thorns, which grew up and choked the plants.

Matthew 13:7

I pulled back the husk from the scrubby, deformed ear of corn. How disappointed I was in the few kernels of corn on the cob; the ear should have been ten to twelve inches long and bursting with at least a hundred kernels of grain or more.

As Dad and I gazed over the field, it appeared most of the stalks bore similar small, deformed ears of corn. We were looking at the results of corn plants having been choked, choked almost to death, by weeds.

The spring had begun with much promise. The soil had tilled easily into a soft plant bed. The sun was shining and the sky was blue as we planted the seed in straight rows across the field. The correct fertilizer to nourish the seed was applied. With eager anticipation, we knew a bountiful harvest was forthcoming. Then the June rains came. Day after day it rained, preventing us from cultivating the weeds out of the corn. Oh, the rains were great for the corn. It grew rapidly, but so did the weeds. The ground was too muddy to cultivate, and pre-emergent herbicides (chemicals that kill weeds as they sprout) had yet to be discovered.

In July and August, it turned dry. As the corn and weeds competed for moisture and nutrients, it seemed that the weeds won.

Now it was October. Instead of a bountiful harvest as hoped for, Dad and I silently looked over a field barely worth the cost of harvesting.

Finally the silence was broken by Dad. "Son, you remember the parable of the sower and seed?"

"Yes, Dad, I do," I replied.

Dad continued. "Well, this field of corn is a classic example of the truths Jesus was teaching in the parable." (See Matthew 13:5-8; Mark 4:3-8; Luke 8:5-8.)

As I reflected upon what I remembered from a recent sermon and the parable, I remembered that some seeds were sown among the seeds of thorns. As both sprouted and grew, the good seeds or plants had been eventually choked out.

"Son, you have seen how hard the ground is packed at the entrance (gate) into the field, how the seed doesn't sprout and the birds eat it. You have also seen how seeds sprout and grow only for a short period of time where the soil is rocky and shallow. Now you are looking at not just a corn crop failure, but a physical example of a spiritual truth: the truth that sin (weeds) in a life can choke out any, and even all, potential spiritual fruit." Dad studied the ground, deep in thought. "Do you remember how the nation of Israel continually lost God's blessings and were punished even into captivity, when all manner of sin was allowed to grow among them— the sins of greed, lust, idolatry, thievery, murder, grumbling, complaining, etc? And, Son, what is even worse, all these weeds will produce thousands of seeds that we will be fighting for years. These weeds are a perfect picture of what James 1:13-15 tells us: that sin which is allowed to grow in a life chokes out any spiritual fruit, climaxing in even death."

The "weeds of sin" in people's lives became so great in Noah's time that it brought the consequences of a universal flood, with only Noah and his family being spared. The "weeds of sin" cost Lot a portion of his family. The "weeds of sin" cost Achan his life and the lives of his family (Joshua 7). The "weeds of sin" brought God's periodic judgment upon the nation of Israel, especially in the time of the Judges. The "weeds of sin" caused many to die during the Exodus of God's people from Egypt to the Promised Land. The "weeds of sin" under Solomon caused the nation of Israel to divide. This is only the beginning of the biblical illustrations of the "weeds of sin."

With sadness, Dad finished his thoughts. "Son, do you remember how one of our neighbors allowed sin to grow in his life that eventually led to his death by suicide? Let this field of corn choked by weeds teach you how sin can choke a spiritual life into unfruitfulness."

As I have weeded many gardens and fields over the years, I have learned the best time to remove weeds is when they are small, and the best way to remove weeds is to pull out the roots to totally stop future growth. Weeds that are allowed to grow often develop a large root system, making it almost impossible to remove them. It is no different with sin. The best method of eradicating sin from one's life is when the sin is small. Remove it by the roots so it won't re-grow and devastate a life. When weeds, or sins, are only broken off and not pulled out by the roots, they will re-grow.

Proverbs 28:13 teaches us that "He who conceals his sin does not prosper, but whoever confesses and renounces them (pulls them out by the roots) finds mercy."

"If we confess our sins, he is faithful and just to forgive us our sins, and to cleanse (pull out by the roots) us from all unrighteousness." John 1:9 (KJV)

Recently a woman asked me why my flower beds are so free of weeds. I explained to her that I watch daily for weeds and when they appear, I pull them out. I also explained that once the flowers are mature, they shade the ground so that few weeds sprout and grow. Active, full spiritual growth and maturity shades our hearts and minds so that sin has no sunlight in which to flourish.

The weed-filled corn field I saw as a boy, I now see reflected in our country, our culture, our churches (yes, even churches), and our families in the form of spiritual unfruitfulness. I see spiritual barrenness caused by the stranglehold of the deceitfulness of riches, sensual pleasures, and lustful desires.

The best way to eradicate the "weeds" of sin from our lives is succinctly stated by the Psalmist, "Thy Word have I hid in my heart, that I might not sin against thee" (Psalm 119:11, KJV). "The law of God is in his heart; none of his steps shall slide (slip into ruin)" (Psalm 37:31, KJV). The teaching and preaching of the Word of God is like a pre-emergent herbicide. It keeps the weeds of sin from sprouting and growing.

How is the condition of the "field" of your heart? Is it full of spiritual "weeds"? Or is it "weed-free" because you have cultivated with the Word of God?

> As I surveyed the flower bed,
> I saw a weed ever so small.
> Being lazy I passed it by,
> And within in a few weeks it had grown so
>   tall.

> I shall put it out,
> Surely it will be mere play.
> But, the now deeply rooted
> Weed was there to stay.

> I pulled, yanked and sweated
> As from the earth I tore it free.
> But the gaping hole in the
> Earth was there for all to see.

> As I cooled down under the shade of a tree,
> I realized the weed was a picture of me.
> I had allowed little sins of me to grow.
> I had not allowed God's Word to be a
>   cleansing flow.

Finally I repented of my sin with much
   remorse
And a loving, forgiving God removed it with
   great force.

The removal of the big weed
Did the earth mar.
So also the removal of sin,
left on my heart a scar.

   —Author

DISTRESSED, BUT HOPEFUL

"HELP, I AM IN PAIN. PLEASE SEND THE PERFECT ARBORIST."

We know that the whole creation has been groaning
as in the pains of childbirth right up to the present time.

Romans 8:22

"The tree is distressed because it has to wait for Jesus to come."

In an instant, my granddaughter's words turned my mind to Romans 8. Never before had I fully made the connection between the Fall of mankind and the whole of all God's creation.

It had been a brutally hot and dry summer, and record high temperatures were set on several days. I was responsible for many thousands of plants at a large plant nursery where I was employed as their garden specialist; at a professional business as landscaper and gardener; and at my home—day after day, week after week, I had struggled to keep them alive.

I was watering plants often before daylight and after dark. The thirsty, sometimes wilted plants were continually under stress and cried out for relief. At times it seemed I was losing the battle to keep plants, including shrubs and trees, healthy and blooming. All of God's creation, both plant and man, was groaning under the burden of man's Fall into sin, as I will explain later.

In early September some cooler weather and refreshing rains came, lifting much of the heavy burden. On a planned vacation trip that took my wife and I through Knoxville (Tennessee), we had brunch with some of our family. As we walked from the restaurant, my son shared how one of his trees was distressed from the hot, dry summer. He went on to explain some recommendations that an arborist had made to relieve the stress. At this point, my granddaughter made her observation about the tree waiting for Jesus to come, which sent me hastily to Romans 8.

Romans 8:18-30! What a marvelous passage of Scripture! More often than not, we focus our attention on the 28th and 29th verses. However, as verses 28 and 29 reveal to us the sovereignty of God, so do the earlier verses reveal how, when Adam and Eve sinned, all of creation came under the curse of sin. Romans 8:22 states, "We know that the whole creation has been groaning as in the pains of childbirth right up to the present time." Dr. Charles Ryrie shares this insight about verses 20-22: "After Adam sinned, God was obliged to subject the creation to futility so that man in his sinful state might retain some measure of dominion over creation."

Simply stated, nature was involved in man's Fall; she will be emancipated when man is fully restored.

Verses 20 and 21 also tell us that creation (nature) was subjected to frailty, futility, frustration, and decay; condemned not because of some intentional fault on its part, but by the will of Him, yet with hope for redemption.

When Jesus comes again and establishes His millennial reign, all of His creation will be set free from its corruption.

Creation, as all mankind, longs to return to the Garden of Eden. There, the weather was perfect. No sprinkling systems or hoses were needed, as the plants were perfectly watered (probably from an underground river containing nutrients so no fertilizer was needed), the soil was perfect in its texture and structure, the plants that loved sun had the right amount, and the shade-loving plants thrived under the taller trees and shrubs. What a paradise it must have been!

My son's problem with his tree reminded me of many years earlier when I walked through a grove of dying Dutch Elm trees. As a boy growing up, I enjoyed the beauty and shade of the stately Dutch Elm, often playing around, in, and under them. Then it struck! The dreaded Dutch Elm disease. There was no fungicide or Insecticide to stop this quickly-spreading disease. I just wanted to take a big bucket of soapy water and wash the trees to stop the dreaded disease. Within a few years, our beautiful trees were dead. With heavy hearts, we cut them down, and the wood became firewood to heat our home. Millions of trees throughout the country were lost due to this disease.

At the time, I didn't connect the loss of my shady playground with Romans 8. But I witnessed the pallor of death because of the Fall of all God's creation.

Although we had no cure for Dutch Elm disease and its ravages, God provides us a cure from the disease and ravages of sin, through Jesus Christ and His Word. Psalm 119:9 (KJV) states, "Wherewithal shall a young man cleanse his way? By taking heed thereto according to thy word." I John 1:7,9 (KJV) says, "But if we walk in the light, as he is in the light, we have fellowship one with another, and the blood of Jesus Christ, his Son, cleanseth us from all sin. If we confess our sins, he is faithful and just to forgive us our sins, and to cleanse us from all unrighteousness."

The passage in Romans reveals to us that all of God's creation suffered, and continues to suffer, from the Fall. However, the same passage gives all creation hope for the future. Like man, all of creation is crying out and longing for God's redemption. "Let the sea resound, and all that is in it; let the fields be jubilant, and everything in them! Then the trees of the forest will sing, they will sing for joy before the LORD, for he comes to judge the earth" (I Chronicles 16:32-33, NIV).

How fitting it should be—trees that reminded me of the Fall of creation also remind me of this magnificent gift from the Creator, which provides the bookends of the Word of God, the writing of which spans around 1,500 years. The first reference to a tree is found in Genesis 2:9, the Tree of Life, and the last is in Revelation 22:2,14—again, the Tree of Life. The Bible itself contains more references to trees than to any other living thing, except people. From the best cedars of Lebanon, a portion of the temple was built. It was a wooden cross, made from a tree that God created, on which Jesus died to pay for our sins.

Thanks, granddaughter, for reminding me why all of God's creation suffers from sin's curse, and also of the blessed hope of eternal redemption and perfect restoration.

Let fields rejoice, and everything
That springs up from the earth;
Then woods and every tree shall sing
With gladness and with mirth
—*Old Scottish Psalter*

DEMONIC POWER

"Demon-Possessed Pigs"

*When the demons came out of the man, they went into the
pigs, and the herd rushed down the steep bank into the lake
and was drowned.*

Luke 8:33

"That pig is demon-possessed!" my wife of less than a year
exclaimed. As the pig came down the aisle from the
show ring, my wife had attempted to herd it into its pen. The 250-
pound pig had lowered its head, brushed aside the wooden herding
panel, and knocked her over. I didn't dare laugh at the misfortunes
of my new bride (although others who saw it did). "That pig needs
to be drowned, just like you read about in the Bible," she muttered
as I helped her up and brushed the dirt from her clothes.

"Now, honey, let's not be hasty in bringing about the pig's form
of execution. There are better ways," I responded. "In a few days
we can have it butchered and enjoy ham, bacon, sausage, and pork
chops. Then you will have your revenge. If the pig is demon-
possessed as you claim, it will depart for places unknown when the
pig is butchered. Shortly thereafter, we can have a sausage biscuit

for breakfast; a bacon, lettuce and tomato sandwich for lunch; and a brown sugar-cured ham for supper." My words, for the moment, seemed to sooth her embarrassment and hurt.

Someone coined the phrase "hog heaven." It supposedly describes a person's feelings when they are experiencing a time of great delight and happiness. I don't know where or what "hog heaven" is, but at the time my wife had anything but heavenly thoughts.

Three of the four Gospel writers record Jesus casting out the demon(s) and allowing them to enter into the herd of swine. So it had to be an event of significant importance.

For many years, our needed machinery repairs were taken to a local Christian blacksmith and repair shop. Dean, the owner, was not only talented with his hands, but also had the God-given ability to cast out demons. Almost weekly, people would call him to come cast a demon out of a family member or friend. Sometimes Dean would ask me if I wanted to go along with him when he was called upon to cast out a demon. I always declined. His stories of encountering demons were so vivid and scary that I didn't want any part of getting that close to any kind of demonic activity, especially when he would describe in detail about strange voices coming from inside a person; how people would be thrown violently to the floor and then writhe in pain; and how one family would need to hold a person down so they would not hurt themselves or others.

His encounters would make the best spooky Halloween movie or story ever produced. Although I liked to think I was as tough as John Wayne or Jimmy Stewart, this was one area where I wanted no part.

Dean was very Christ-like and a man of much prayer. He often said, "Unless you're prayed up, you will never have the anointed power to cast out demons."

The human finite mind can't really grasp just how powerful Satan or one of his demons can be. When I first heard the story of the maniac and how Jesus cast out the demon(s), I figured they must be really powerful. Those demons, when allowed to enter the herd of swine, caused them to jump into the lake and commit suicide. That is powerful.

The story of what Jesus did sure left me with several questions that no one seemed able to answer. Why did Jesus allow the demons to enter the herd of swine? Why couldn't the demons just float in space? (Later I learned they needed a place of habitation). Was the owner of the swine a Jew or a Gentile? If the owner was a Jew, was he raising those pigs to sell to Gentiles since Jews were forbidden to eat pork? Why were the local people so upset about the loss of the herd, rather than rejoicing that Jesus had set a man free from the demon's power? Human nature has not changed. People still complain more than they praise.

In my lifetime, I have sadly and with concern learned that there are still demon-possessed people today. Yes, even in the USA, which is supposedly a civilized nation, not just in so-called "third world countries."

Our society is increasingly occupied with the occult. Millions each day read and believe their horoscope rather than God's Word. The celebration of Halloween becomes increasingly satanic-influenced. Thousands each month seek the advice of palm readers, so-called spiritual mediums, and sorcerers. Whole gangs of youth use devilish symbols to identify themselves and invite Satan himself to be their leader. Thousands each year commit suicide, perhaps under the influence of, or actually possessed by, demons.

People, including youths, have confessed they have committed horrendous crimes because Satan told them to do it. Magazines, books, movies, and television show portray Satan and his demons as beings who have no more power than a human being. People wear T-shirts that say "The devil made me do it." They openly flaunt their ignorance of their own sin nature and the evil power of Satan. How tragic.

Scripture has 164 direct references to Satan as the devil, as well as many indirect references. There has been, in the past and ever increasingly today, a major spiritual battle between God and Satan, good and evil, darkness and light, lies and truth, wickedness and righteousness. Sadly, even tragically, few Christians recognize the scope of this spiritual battle, and the only way one can overcome any type of demonic influence is in the name and blood of Jesus, prayer, and the Word of God. Jesus set the example when he refuted the devil by using His Father's (and His) Word when He was tempted forty days and nights in the wilderness.

I love to read the accounts in the Old Testament of godly kings who destroyed the temples, altars, satanic idols of false gods, etc. I would have loved to help them. I can picture myself with an axe or sledgehammer in hand and a stick of "dynamite" in the other hand, destroying Satan's strongholds.

Paul, writing to the Ephesians (6:10-18) told us to put on the whole armor of God in order to withstand all Satan and his demons throw at us. Satan is the father and master of murder, deceit, lies, greed, depression, defeat, destruction, discouragement, false imitation; he is a thief, ravenous as a roaring lion masquerading as an angel of light, and instigator of all manner of debauchery. Satan and his demonic activity and influence, coupled with man's sinful nature, erupts into a myriad of sins. The root cause of man's lust, troubles, pride, greed, and diseases is sin. Sin will cost a person more than they want to pay, take them farther than they want to go, and keep them longer than they want to stay.

It would be great if fathers, local church leaders, and national leaders, like the godly kings of Israel of old, destroyed the "temples of Satan."

Do you and your family have on the whole armor of God? I trust and pray you do. Without the whole armor of God, Satan and his satanic influence will destroy your family.

SUNDAY AFTERNOONS

"FOOD, FAMILY, AND FUN"

*Keep the sabbath day to sanctify it, as the LORD thy God
hath commanded thee. Six days thou shalt labour, and do all
thy work: But the seventh day is the Sabbath of the LORD
thy God: in it thou shalt not do any work, thou, nor thy son,
nor thy daughter, nor thy manservant, nor thy maidservant,
nor thine ox, nor thine ass, nor any of thy cattle, nor thy
stranger that is within thy gates; that thy manservant and thy
maidservant may rest as well as thou. And remember that thou
wast a servant in the land of Egypt, and that the LORD thy
God brought thee out thence through a mighty hand and by a
stretched out arm; therefore the LORD thy God commanded
thee to keep the sabbath day.*

Deuteronomy 5:12-15 (KJV)

"Come on, everybody, let's go play softball!" I called out to
my brothers, sister, and Dad. "Fred (younger brother),
you go invite the neighbor kids to join us. Dick (another brother),
get the empty sacks out of the barn for bases. Arlene (sister), you get
the bat and ball. Let's go! It will be fun!"

I was the expediter and provided the enthusiasm. With great excitement, we all went about our duties in anticipation of our Sunday afternoon ball game.

Sunday was a day for church, followed by a scrumptious Sunday noon dinner as only Mom could prepare. Then, many of the afternoons were spent playing softball in the spring and summer, football in the fall, and good old Hoosier barn basketball in the winter. The only exception to our Sunday afternoon games was when Dad and Mom loaded us into the car to go visit relatives. Oh, we grumbled and complained, but we still went. We kids felt it was a real waste of prime playing time just to hear the men talk about politics and the women discuss cooking, sewing, etc.

The only time we looked forward to going to Grandpa and Grandma Gordon's was if we knew Uncle Evart would be there. Someone would challenge him on his beliefs in—and the actions of—the Democratic Party, which usually led to a most spirited argument.

After the usual ball game, we would do chores, eat a light supper of sandwiches, leftovers from dinner, and popcorn, a family favorite. Then to evening church we went, followed by bedtime.

It was a day of worship, great Sunday dinners, family times, and mostly fun-filled afternoons and rest for Dad and Mom.

Sixty years later, as I reflect back upon these Sundays and compare them to the Sundays of today's culture, I am very sad.

The Scriptures, both Old and New Testament, make it very clear that the Lord's Day is for worship, family, and rest. In Scriptures there are 167 references to the Sabbath and how it should be spent. God gave clear instructions concerning how man should treat the

Sabbath—our Sunday—and the serious consequences when violated (even death for violators). Of all the Ten Commandments, the one to honor the Sabbath is probably the most misunderstood, misused, and widely ignored. A thorough search of Scripture reveals one "do" and one "don't" concerning the Sabbath. The one thing we are told to do is gather together to worship (Hebrews 10:25). The don't is work—God rules out any kind of work on the Sabbath, except that which preserves human life or an act of human kindness. With cessation of work, there is a blessed rest.

There is a marvelous example of man's responsibility to cease from work on the Sabbath. In Exodus chapter 16, the grumbling Israelites wanted food. God gave them heavenly manna. They were told to gather only what they needed for one day. When they gathered more than they needed, it spoiled (which involved disgusting maggots). However, on the day before the Sabbath, they gathered enough for two days. On the Sabbath, instead of being rotten, the manna was sweeter than the day before.

Patrick Klingman, in his book Finding Rest, states, "Did God bless the six days and make them holy? No, in Genesis 2:3 God blessed the seventh day and made it holy, because that was the day He rested from His work. From the beginning of the world then, rest has value because God gave it value by His blessing. It is not a practical 'activity,' but a 'HOLY ONE'" (emphasis mine) (page 21).

Although God spoke of what He created the first six days of creation as being good, even very good, it was the seventh day He made holy.

Failing to honor Sunday as a day of worship and rest has an enormous negative impact upon both physical and mental health.

Many health studies have positively shown that two-thirds of physician office visits are stress related. The nonstop, frantic pace of our culture has led all the way from headaches, to major heart disease, and even death.

Although the biblical Sabbaths are now our Sundays, the basic principles remain the same. Sunday should be a time when a family (or individual) worships together, eats together, plays together and, yes, even rests together.

As I look over our communities—our nation—I see more and more businesses open (not counting hospitals, health clinics, which are of necessity open), forcing millions to work on Sunday. The god of these businesses is money; i.e., the "bottom line," and they think they must be open on Sunday. Not so! Truett Cathy, founder of Chick-fil-A (and thousands of other businessmen) have proved this false; they have been successful without being open on Sundays.

Increasingly, I have heard people whose places of employment are open on Sundays say, "I wish I did not have to work on Sunday; I wish I could spend my Sundays in church and with my family."

Millions of people believe they would not survive if only the necessary health care facilities were open on Sundays. Nonsense! They could buy the gas, food, repairs, etc. on Friday and Saturday (or any other day of the week), just as my (and your) parents, grandparents, and millions of others did in the past.

Our ancestors showed by example that Sabbaths should be a time of contemplation – an incubator for thought and wisdom; evaluation – of God's goodness and past blessings upon us; restoration – of body, mind and soul; celebration – of all our future blessings through Jesus Christ our Lord and His creation; inspiration – to renew our vision for God's work; separation – from the material-istic culture of the day; communion – with God and His Word; and fellowship – with family, neighbors, etc.

What would our communities, our country, be like if we returned to following God's plan for His special day? I believe there would be a revival of true worship, of family togetherness and unity, lower crime rates, quieter and more peaceful communities and, yes, even a stronger economy.

How do you and your family spend your Sundays?

Blessed is the nation whose God is the LORD,
the people he chose for his inheritance.

Psalm 33:12

CONCLUSION

I trust as you have read this book you have been challenged, convicted, sobered, and entertained. I pray that you have come to understand that biblical principles never change. God has said that He is the same yesterday, today, and forever. His Word, which has withstood every human effort to destroy it, is as relevant to our lives today as when it was first written.

By now you may have sensed that, to some degree, I long for and would like to return (at least in part) to the "good old days." I can assure you I have no desire to return to some things; e.g., having to use the outhouse on cold, wintry days due to the lack of indoor plumbing; or waking up to a cold, chilly house because the fire in the wood-burning furnace went out at about midnight.

Yes, I do long for the days when the family unit was the backbone of the community, the nation, and the church. For sure I long for the time when a man's word was his bond; the days when large agreements were consummated with a handshake, compared to lengthy written contracts requiring a lawyer to write them; a time when windows and doors were left unlocked day and night because without fear of an intruder (compare that with now when we need to have double, even triple, locks plus sophisticated alarm systems); and a time when the culture and society were decidedly more moral, wholesome, and ethical.

Certainly there were criminals, immorality, and sinful behavior when I was growing up. Yes, there were evil people doing devilish deeds, but it was not nearly as evident as today nor so openly flaunted.

Early in this book, I spoke of a book titled They Had Everything but Money. The book is filled with human interest stories of how people survived the Great Depression of the 1930s. The stories are of love, sharing of all resources (money, food, clothing, etc.) as people struggled to survive.

Today many people have made money their god. They have money and all kinds of material things, and nothing else. Our attics, basements, garages, and closets are overflowing with stuff, stuff, and more stuff, and yet millions of homes are empty of what matters most—empty of love, of caring one for another, of generosity, of laughter, and of biblical morality.

My heart is broken when I see the crime-infested, drug-addicted, entertainment-crazy, corrupt, and immoral society in which we live, especially when I see how our children and young people have been drawn into it. There are tears in my eyes as I think of the millions of broken homes that have wreaked untold, immeasurable havoc upon the children.

But, Praise God! There is hope. Jesus Christ still redeems and restores the lost sinners. He still is able to resurrect and empower struggling families. He is still able to rekindle the flames of revival and renewal not only in our homes, but also in our churches, businesses, and nation.

I trust this book has made you think about your personal and family life.

May God richly bless you and meet all your material and spiritual needs as only He can do. By God's grace, may you be a godly parent to your children. I am deeply grateful for my godly parents, as your children will be also.

ABOUT THE AUTHOR

JIM GEYER OFFERS THE WISDOM he gleaned from his experience on the farm, pictured below, in this book *Dad & Mom's Country Wisdom: Everything I Know about the Bible I Learned Down on the Farm.*

For more information about
Jim Geyer
&

Dad & Mom's Country Wisdom
please visit, call or write:

jjgeyer@~~charter.net~~ *outlook. com*

~~(864) 288-3307~~

574- 354 - 1914

....

For more information about
AMBASSADOR INTERNATIONAL
please visit:

www.ambassador-international.com
@AmbassadorIntl
www.facebook.com/AmbassadorIntl